SURVIVING
ADOLESCENTS
2.0

Dr Michael Carr-Gregg is a child and adolescent psychologist, broadcaster, a well-respected speaker and one of Australia's leading authorities on teenage behaviour and parenting. In 1985 he founded CanTeen, the acclaimed cancer patients' support group for teenagers in New Zealand and Australia. He is the consultant psychologist to many schools and national organisations, and has written twelve books on parenting adolescents.

Elly Robinson is a researcher, writer and mother who began her career as a youth worker. Since then she has worked to promote the use of evidence in practice with children, young people and families. She has a Graduate Diploma in Adolescent Health and a Master of Public Health from the University of Melbourne.

BOOKS BY DR MICHAEL CARR-GREGG

Surviving Adolescents

Real Wired Child

When to Really Worry

Surviving Step-Families

Beyond Cyberbulling

Strictly Parenting

The Princess Bitchface Syndrome 2.0
(with Elly Robinson)

The Prince Boofhead Syndrome
(with Elly Robinson)

SURVIVING ADOLESCENTS 2.0

2.0

DR MICHAEL CARR-GREGG
AND ELLY ROBINSON

PENGUIN LIFE

UK | USA | Canada | Ireland | Australia
India | New Zealand | South Africa | China

Penguin Books is part of the Penguin Random House group of companies
whose addresses can be found at global.penguinrandomhouse.com.

Penguin
Random House
Australia

First published by Penguin Random House Australia Pty Ltd, 2018

1 3 5 7 9 10 8 6 4 2

Text copyright © Michael Carr-Gregg and Elly Robinson, 2018

The moral rights of the authors have been asserted.

Cover design by Alex Ross © Penguin Random House Australia Pty Ltd
Cover photograph by Antonio Guillem/Getty Images
Typeset in Adobe Caslon by Midland Typesetters, Australia
Printed and bound in Australia by Griffin Press, an accredited ISO AS/NZS 14001
Environmental Management Systems printer.

A catalogue record for this
book is available from the
National Library of Australia

ISBN 978 0 14378 466 1

penguin.com.au

Contents

Preface

I never cease to be amazed by young people and what they can achieve. Take, for example, teen adventurer Jade Hameister. In early 2018, at 16 years old, Jade became the youngest person to complete the 'polar hat-trick' by adding a 37-day journey to reach the South Pole to previous trips across Greenland and to the North Pole. Or Deng Adut, who was taken from his mother at around 6 years old and forced to fight as a child soldier for the Sudan People's Liberation Army. At 12 years old he almost bled to death after being shot several times. At 14, he and his brother reached Australia. He knew little English and had barely attended school, but Adut eventually graduated with a Bachelor of Laws and became a defence lawyer in Western Sydney, where he now does much of his work pro bono for the Sudanese community.

These are extreme examples, but they serve to illustrate just how amazing adolescents can be when they put their minds to something, regardless of the fact that they may have grown up in circumstances of pervasive adversity.

In my work as an adolescent psychologist, I regularly see young people who are struggling with depression, anxiety, body image and self-harm, and I often need reminding that there are plenty of adolescents who are happily and successfully navigating the journey towards adulthood.

This book focuses on what you as a parent need to know about the adolescent journey in the 21st century to help your teenagers – and you – thrive. It incorporates the latest research on what creates happy and resilient young people. Of course, the irony of being a parent of a teenager is that by the time you are experienced, your job is done and you are unemployed! This book seeks to fast-track your learning of the key competencies, so everyone benefits in the years that matter.

SO WHY WRITE A NEW EDITION OF *SURVIVING ADOLESCENTS*?

Findings from a range of studies and reports in recent years that have examined young people's mental health and wellbeing give us good reason to increase our focus on the adolescent years. For example, the results from Young Minds Matter, a national survey of over 6000 Australian families in 2013–14, showed the following in the twelve months prior to the survey:

- One in seven 4–17-year-olds had experienced a mental disorder. This equates to more than half a million children and young people.
- One in thirteen 11–17-year-olds had a major depressive disorder. The highest rate (one in five)

was for girls aged 16–17 years, of whom one in twenty had also attempted suicide.

- Almost half of young people with depressive disorders experienced a severe impact on their lives, including a high number of school absences.
- One in five adolescents (12–17 years) suffered from high to very high levels of psychological distress.
- One in twelve adolescents had self-harmed in the previous twelve months. Self-harm is far more common among young women compared to young men.
- One in thirteen adolescents had seriously considered suicide, and one-third (or more than 40 000) of these had attempted suicide.

The Australian Bureau of Statistics, which releases information on causes of death each year, reported that in 2015, suicide rates among young Australians were at their highest level in ten years, with female suicide rates for 15–19-year-olds doubling in this period. Rates of suicide and self-harm are particularly high for young people with an experience of mental illness, LGBTIQ young people, young people living in rural and remote areas and Aboriginal and Torres Strait Islander young people.

School and family stressors also contribute to mental health disorders. The Young Minds Matter survey found that mental disorders were particularly common in families that faced other challenges, such as unemployment or family separation. When it comes to education stressors, a study by the UNSW School of Education in

2015 confirmed what many teachers and parents already knew – Year 12 in particular is highly stressful for many students. Almost half reported anxiety at a level of clinical concern, which is nearly double the population norm, and one in seven reported 'extremely severe' levels of anxiety. Things don't seem to improve once students move on to university, either. The National Tertiary Student Wellbeing Survey, conducted in 2016, showed that one in three higher education students (16–25 years) reported that thoughts of suicide or self-harm affected their studies, and two-thirds self-reported high to very high levels of psychological stress.

It's as if, in the past ten years or so, our teenagers have experienced a seemingly relentless emotional siege. This is a calamitous picture of failing mental health compared to previous generations. It seems like risk factors are swamping any available protective factors in young people's lives, as both boys and girls are carpet-bombed with social media and advertising images that undermine self-esteem, influence food choices and erode self-confidence.

The efforts of parents, schools and other professional groups to offset these risk factors for mental illness are struggling to keep up with this constant barrage. Just when a young person's identity and sense of self is at its most fragile, they potentially face more judgement and rejection than ever, courtesy of social media giants such as Instagram and Snapchat, the digital colosseums in which they engage daily in a battle of the selfies.

Like never before, we need parents, carers and other adults to have the skills, knowledge and strategies to provide this generation's young people with the love, stability, routine and predictability they need. We need adults to model self-reliance and self-acceptance, and to provide a space where young people can express their anxieties and worries without fear of judgement.

To help me write this book, I have enlisted one of Australia's most respected and brilliant translational researchers to help me condense and explain the vast clinical and academic evidence base about adolescents and parents. Elly Robinson is not just a friend, parent of a teenager and a co-author of two of my other books, but she is simply a genius at taking convoluted research and transforming it into information that we can all use and understand.

Elly and I believe that the task of supporting the health and wellbeing of this generation of teenagers requires a new skill set: for everyone who comes into contact with teenagers to understand the developmental psychology of adolescence, the stages of adolescence, how the teen brain develops, how to manage risk factors and build resilience, and how to communicate and negotiate effectively with pre-teens and teenagers. It requires us to apply this skills and knowledge base to help young people manage their use of technology, social media and relationships, bullying and substance use, sex and sexual relationships and the many other challenges that will cross their paths in these critical years.

There is no doubt the early years are critical to health and wellbeing, but political attention has been transfixed by the early childhood years for too long. Infants and preschoolers are far easier to focus on than teenagers, who can at times seem almost universally unlikeable and barely tolerable. By focusing on the early years so intently, the risk is that society thinks the job is done by mid primary school. By neglecting the importance of the adolescent phase of development, we fail to finish the job we started.

Adolescence is the second most risky growth and developmental period next to infancy. It's time we recognised and responded to it as such, or else I fear that those alarming figures I shared will continue to rise.

Introduction

When my first son was a newborn, I thought that parenting was quite a slog: the endless nappies, the sleepless nights and that baby vomit smell that seemed to permeate all my clothing . . . but little did I know, there were greater challenges to come. There is an Italian saying '. . . *Piccoli bambini, mal di testa; grandi bambini, mal di cuore,*' which translates as 'little children, headache; big children, heartache'.

WELCOME TO ADOLESCENCE

The 2016 Australian Bureau of Statistics (ABS) Census showed that there were more than 2.8 million 10–19-year-olds living in Australia; 42 000 more than recorded in the last census in 2011. That's a lot of preteens and teenagers, Slurpees and mobile phones in hand, to be tripping over in your local shopping centre. Most of this cohort will be at school currently, but soon many of them will be at university, searching for jobs or a part of the trend in Australia of youth unemployment or underemployment, which has remained stubbornly high since the global financial crisis of 2008. Increasingly these young people remain in the family home and parents continue to play a significant role in their life (see Chapter 3 for more on young adults at home).

The closer the proximity of the teenage years, the easier it is to come across tales of woe that highlight parents' fear, uncertainty and general negativity towards this period in their children's lives. In 2013, the UK online parenting network Netmums asked 1000 mothers and fathers about their experiences of parenting. More than half of parents said that dealing with teenagers was more testing than caring for a newborn baby, and almost a quarter said that they found their children most troublesome at age 13, followed by ages 11, 12 and (you guessed it) 14. Surging hormones, laziness, growing sexual awareness, body image and new technology were all named as contributing to the difficulties in parenting. However, the good news was that things tended to improve by the time their children turned 17 – only six short years in all!

A study in 2017 by the Parenting Research Centre in Victoria found that parents of 13–18-year-olds were less likely to agree that they had the skills necessary to be a good parent to their child compared to when their children were younger. Parents were also more likely to feel that they were more often critical of their teenagers than their younger children, and the extent to which parents argued with or yelled at their children about their behaviour or attitude also rose with age.

These findings are entirely unsurprising. Of all the

events that occur in a family's life cycle, adolescence is the most likely to test the flexibility, tolerance and relevance of an existing bag of parenting tricks. The quiet, compliant child of recent memory appears to transform overnight and is faced with a variety of psychological hoops to jump through that are simply incomparable to the relatively straightforward adolescence of their parents. One could argue that we as a society are losing it when it comes to managing our own emotional lives and training our teenagers to manage theirs.

A big part of the problem is the increasing lack of psychological mooring posts for young people in our communities. As teenagers, many of us grew up with an affiliation to a particular suburb, sporting club, community group or church, which allowed us the opportunity to engage in activities away from the prying eyes of our parents. These alliances have become less common, with the advent of technology and greater mobility related to employment opportunities and a global economy. Many families are left on their own to raise teenagers without the wisdom and experience they might have derived from past generations, or the supervision and monitoring of caring adults in the broader community. Research studies from around the world say that one of the most important protective factors in the lives of young people is a close relationship with a supportive adult, yet we seem to be losing the ability to facilitate these relationships.

Most parents I know struggle to generate the psychological sinew required, are time poor and often don't have the energy or even the inclination to attend information sessions held on freezing evenings, let alone read a weighty treatise on developmental psychology. So in this book we have set out to provide a concise guide to surviving daily life with adolescents. I'm a big believer in trying to keep advice to parents as realistic and practical as possible. For this reason, as well as suggesting some strategic approaches, I have also included some fairly basic tips. These may seem obvious, but I know from personal and professional experience that they are things that are all too easy to forget in the heat of battle. After all, forewarned is forearmed!

Although raising young people can be full of challenges, especially when they seem to constantly make decisions that fly in the face of common sense, there are few things in this world more satisfying than surveying the final product. Despite the developmental challenges adolescents encounter, many demonstrate formidable grit and determination and end up making us all immensely proud. The good news is that the majority of teenagers will navigate adolescence and remain generally happy, healthy and well. This book will help you understand the important role you play, and how best to play it, to ensure your teenager is one of the majority.

Part 1

All about adolescents

Many parents look forward to the teenage years with the same level of enthusiasm reserved for doing their annual taxes. The fact that teenagers don't enjoy a favourable public profile is somewhat to blame for this. Word association tests with your average adult in the street are likely to elicit adjectives such as irresponsible, immoral, violent, narcissistic, self-absorbed, materialistic and reckless. It's a perception that is unfair, wrong and exceptionally annoying to young people. Ask any teenager what it is like to be regularly followed around a shopping centre by the security staff, presumably for the crime of being a teenager. Or how it feels when adults get annoyed with you or tell you off for being loud in a public space, even though teenagers are rarely provided with youth-friendly spaces of their own.

Part of the problem with negative stereotypes is that they can be a self-fulfilling prophecy. One US study found that students in Grade 6 and 7 whose mothers expected risky and rebellious behaviour were duly rewarded within the twelve months following the initial survey. By thinking that this type of behaviour is normal for teenagers (regardless of whether one's own teenager has a history that suggests they are likely to engage in risk behaviours) parents add to the chorus of voices that make teenagers feel different or unusual if they don't take risks or break laws.

We miss out on the opportunity to be a significant source of support and guidance for teenagers when we constantly treat them with fear, mistrust and disdain. Many teenagers are smart, driven and engaging – they just need opportunity and understanding to be their best.

The three chapters in this section provide the basis for understanding adolescent development. This information will give you a grounding in some of the biological and psychological reasons as to why teenagers do and say what they do, and how you can use these to help parent them effectively.

Chapter 1
What is adolescence?

Adolescence is a time of rapid transition characterised by a succession of physical, psychological and emotional changes. Teens are no longer children, but not yet adults, and therein lies the root of many teen problems – they want independence and autonomy, but they can still be fragile and needy in the process. They can be funny and entertaining and morose and uncertain all in the space of a couple of hours.

In middle childhood, growth is slow and steady; at puberty, it is anything but this. Young people going through puberty can experience dramatic growth spurts, sometimes growing up to 10 centimetres and gaining around 10 kilograms in one year. This is best reflected in the look of surprise from friends or family who you haven't caught up with in a while, when they're shocked to see an almost-adult, physically developed person standing in front of them instead of the child they remember.

Not all parts of the teenage body develop at the same rate or the same time. The hands and feet are typically the first to grow (just like a puppy!), and as they tend to grow faster than arms and legs, young teenagers can be uncoordinated (so be tolerant if food or drinks are spilled). Around one in five adolescents experience growing pains, usually briefly and at night and typically in the form of aches in the shins, calves or thighs.

PUBERTY

Australian pop singer and actor Rick Springfield once said that next to dying, puberty is likely to be as rough as it gets. Even though Rick is now approaching his 70s, his observation is still relevant for teenagers today. Puberty is associated with transformational physical changes that precede adolescence. During puberty, the brain and pituitary glands release hormones responsible for the development of the reproductive organs in both males and females.

For most Australian girls, puberty is a transition with a fairly standard sequence of physical changes: the ovaries are activated, breasts and body hair develop, and menstruation begins. Girls commonly undergo the growth spurt associated with puberty before or around the same time that they begin to develop sexually. It is often a time of intense adjustment and girls can become hyper-focused on their bodies.

Boys tend to develop sexually first and grow taller and bigger later. Pubertal timing is less well understood in boys, mainly because the age of menarche (first period) in girls is easier to measure in research than the onset of puberty in boys. This is not hard to believe – what teenage boy would want a physical examination of his testicular volume, or to tell a stranger about the timing of his first ejaculation?

Yet stories of body image issues and puberty-related emotional meltdowns in boys who are in mid-to-late primary school are increasingly common. Adrenarche, which is an early stage of puberty that happens around 8–9 years of age, may be responsible for these psychological cataclysms, and boys seem to be particularly affected. Research from the Murdoch Children's Research Institute indicates that the production of androgens such as testosterone at this age may be a more important stage of development than previously thought. Boys who enter adrenarche earlier than their peers show different brain patterns; interestingly, the parents of these boys report a higher incidence of behavioural problems.

Other changes also occur as a result of the increased androgens. Although these changes are less visible than in later puberty, there's still a lot going on – pubic hair follicles become active, the skin becomes greasier and body odour changes. This may explain why a sports team of 8- and 9-year-old boys are noticeably smellier on the school bus home than when they played sport at a younger age.

It's not yet understood why boys appear to be more sensitive to these changes than girls in the middle years. But while there are few external signs to herald the arrival of adrenarche, University of Melbourne's Professor George Patton says we should no longer think of middle childhood as a 'quiet period' of development. Parents need to be fully aware of this, especially with the proliferation of influences at this age such as marketing, online gaming and social media. We need to think far more proactively about ways to create effective educational, social and emotional environments that promote healthy development during these years.

Puberty is being further complicated by the early sexualisation of children and teenagers. Dr Emma Rush, from Charles Sturt University, coined the term 'corporate paedophilia' to describe the actions of corporations who sell products to children in a sexualised way. In her report of the same name, which led to a senate inquiry into issues associated with the sexualisation of children, Dr Rush describes the 'stealing of childhood', in particular the important period between early childhood and adolescence. This premature sexualisation blurs boundaries around who is and isn't sexually mature and makes it difficult for parents and the broader community to understand what is and isn't appropriate.

EARLY PUBERTY

Generally speaking, the age of onset of puberty is now occurring much earlier than in the past (bearing in mind there is considerable variation between children), although recent research suggests that this has started to plateau. The broad consensus is that diet has played a large part in these changes; early puberty is effectively about access to good nutrition (and therefore, technically speaking, the best way to avoid it would be starvation, which is not quite the solution we are after . . .). Other factors, such as family stresses and exposure to chemicals may play a role, but the research isn't all that conclusive in this area. Similarly, it's unclear whether, if the trend in rising obesity is reversed, the trend in early puberty also will reverse.

One recent research study has, however, unmasked an interesting link between social and economic disadvantage and early puberty. Using data from 3700 children collected as part of the Longitudinal Study of Australian Children, researchers at University of Melbourne found that boys from the lowest socio-economic households were four times more likely to reach puberty early, with girls almost twice as likely to do so. Early puberty has been linked to emotional and social problems, including depression and substance abuse, and physical diseases such as heart disease, stroke and various types of cancer. The study therefore highlights early puberty as a possible factor in links between early life disadvantage and poor health outcomes in adulthood.

Earlier onset of puberty also means that physical maturation is no longer in sync with brain development (see pp. 20–21). Those working with adolescents will often be confronted by a young man or woman who is fully developed physically but has the cognitive capability of a 12-year-old. A souped-up car with factory extras, but with an unlicensed driver in charge.

Peter wasn't always big for his age, but his parents had both matured early and they were conscious that, as a result, he might as well. But nothing prepared them for the fact that by age 12, Peter was 168 cm tall, weighed almost as much as his mother, Kim, and was sporting a faint moustache. While all this growth was celebrated in his athletics and footy teams, when she attended his events Kim couldn't help noticing the attention he was getting from some of the older girls. On one occasion, she watched one of these girls, who looked very well physically developed for her age, brush against Peter while they were in conversation. Kim expected Peter to distance himself from the girl but, instead, she was shocked to see he looked somewhat pleased with himself.

Parents like Kim may be worried that a teenager's early physical development will lead to earlier sexual activity. However, thanks to the mismatch in biology and psycho-social development, this is unlikely – growing pubic hair doesn't mean a boy will move directly from Minecraft to mating. An early developer's greatest problem may instead come in the form of one of the ageless issues of our time – bullying of a child who stands out as different from their peers. Early developers are likely to attract attention as the people around them take their growth at face value and assume the individual is older than they are. An early developer may need some more active guidance as they enter the teenage years about what to expect and how to deal with it, including role-playing appropriate responses. For girls, the physical changes of puberty can prompt unwelcome sexualisation of their bodies. If puberty is early, it potentially has implications for a girl's wellbeing that parents need to be attuned to, both in terms of their daughter's self-esteem and the comments or behaviours of those around her.

Early puberty should not be confused with precocious puberty, which is a clinical condition. If development occurs before the age of 8 in a girl or 9 in a boy, seek advice from your GP.

LATE PUBERTY

Siena spent a lot of her free time at school having to listen to her friends talking about their periods. All of her friends had started menstruating – some of them since primary school – but she hadn't. Her best friend had begun teasing her, telling her she was still a 'baby'. Siena was starting to find the whole situation really embarrassing and just wished she would get her period like everyone else.

Late developers may experience significant anxiety about being behind compared to their peers. Siena may need to be assured that puberty occurs at different times, but eventually everyone catches up. Encourage your child to spend time doing things they like and do well to maintain their confidence, and to be accepting about others' experiences, no matter when they happen. If they do, however, get to 14 years old without experiencing any signs of puberty, it's worth booking a check-up with your GP.

Chapter 2

Stages of adolescent development

Am I normal? Who am I? Where am I going? These are the three big questions asked in adolescence, and each question is pondered and tested more or less sequentially as a child moves through the different stages and tasks of adolescence towards independence.

The transition through the adolescent years involves multiple developmental changes across physical, social, emotional, cognitive and identity development realms. This is what it looks like at different stages of the school years and beyond.

LATE PRIMARY SCHOOL (AGES 8-10)
Things begin to change notably at the late primary school stage for most kids. As outlined in the previous chapter, because timing for physical growth varies, some will still look like children while others will have started to develop a more mature body. Children often become more concerned about how they differ from their peers at this stage, and this is compounded by the fact that

puberty most often begins during this stage. Children in early adolescence become acutely aware of their quickly changing bodies and may be apprehensive about their physical appearance, no thanks to the saturation of media images via anything from Instagram to Netflix. Many experience bashfulness, modesty, chronic embarrassment and an absolute obsession with privacy.

Older primary school children start to seek opportunities to increase their independence, and this is developmentally appropriate. They will begin to break emotional bonds with their parents at this stage, which is aided by changes in the brain that increase the child's ability to develop more adult thought processes, such as abstract thinking. A neurological veil is lifted and the child begins to see their adult carers 'warts and all', including discovering they are not infallible and in fact have faults. You may not know whether to expect an eye roll, hug or high-five when you meet them in doorways. Your adolescent's desire to be with their age mates is increasing, and close friends start to become more important than family relationships.

Australian studies on bullying suggest that late primary and early high school are times when bullying is most common. Almost one in three students aged 10–11 years in the Longitudinal Study of Australian Children reported bullying, with name-calling being the most common. Other research shows that bullying has an impact on academic performance, particularly for girls, so parents need to be alert to any signs of bullying at this stage and intervene early. See Chapter 12 for more information on bullying.

EARLY-TO-MID SECONDARY SCHOOL (AGES 11–14)

This is the stage at which the adolescent sense of invincibility kicks in. Adolescents can feel ten feet tall and bulletproof, and the later years of this stage may be the time when engaging in new and more adult behaviours begins, such as drinking alcohol. A hallmark of this period is sexual inquisitiveness, which can be expressed through a keen interest and veneration of movie stars, sporting heroes, singers and online personalities.

Young people in this stage are particularly anxious about their appearance, and believe other people are equally concerned about the way they look. Many worry about personal qualities and 'defects' that are far more noticeable to them than to anyone else.

The increased activity of glands that produce sweats and oils means that body odour and skin problems start to appear, and hair often becomes oilier. These are all big changes that teenagers have to adjust to, and they correspond with what seem like endless hours in front of a mirror or in the bathroom. Wardrobes full of clothes become redundant as 'fit' becomes less about physical size and more about fashion or peer group trends. It's the time when a parent can be driven mad by demands to wash the one pair of jeans (out of the ten that are owned) because the teenager has 'nothing to wear!'

Peers start to become the epicentre of the young person's life as they are faced with the terrible flaws that they perceive their parents have. They are testing out identities and using the symbols of their generation to do so – music, social media, clothes, hairstyles and piercings.

Recent research has pointed to the powerful influence of peers on risk-taking. A US study by Eva Telzer, a neuroscientist at the University of North Carolina, and her colleagues showed that teenagers who are more socially excluded or victimised were likely to take a greater number of risks. By being able to identify who is the most vulnerable, we can help to push them into more positive environments and contexts. It's also important to remember that peers can have *positive* effects on behaviour and can help encourage teenagers to take positive risks.

The early-to-mid secondary student tends to be sensitive to any form of adult control or support, which can often make relationships with parents and carers particularly strained at this time (especially on family holidays!). However, guidance is critical at this age, so keep the lines of communication open, even if it's mainly one way.

MID-TO-LATE SECONDARY SCHOOL (AGES 15–17)

In the mid-to-late secondary school years, teenagers will be pushing harder than ever for independence, which corresponds with an increasing ability to be more mobile without adult supervision. This is the stage where emotional temperatures can rise quickly, as negotiations about attending anything from school to family events to evening parties become far more common. More and more of the teen's friends will be engaging in adult-like experiences, such as drinking alcohol and sexual behaviours, but without necessarily having the full set of skills to manage these situations. Parents and carers will find themselves negotiating important issues with a child who has a larger repertoire of excuses, comparisons and justifications than in previous years, and will need to work together and present a united front. This can be decidedly tricky where parents have separated or divorced (see Chapter 15).

Older teenagers start to feel pressure to live up to the expectations of those around them, especially peers, parents and teachers. Psychologist Lisa Damour states that girls in particular are highly attuned to what others expect of them, and expectations are often higher for girls than for boys. When you add social media to the mix, this magnifies issues such as body image and sexism.

Exploring and forming an identity are critical developmental tasks at this age. Teenagers at this stage are deeply concerned with self-discovery and can be somewhat self-obsessed, which can test the patience of parents and siblings. However, parents shouldn't lose sight of the adolescent's ongoing need to feel that parents are capable of caring for them if life becomes overwhelming. The 14–17-year-old's struggle to dismantle parental authority while knowing that they can come undone if they are *too* successful at pushing parents away is the classic adolescent paradox. Parents need to continue to create a sense of routine and availability for the teen. This can be highly challenging in separated families or where a parent is unable or unwilling to continue to engage in parenting. However, even well-intentioned parents can start to 'check out' at this age because their child appears to be coping.

YOUNG/EMERGING ADULTHOOD (AGES 18–25)

Psychologist Jeffrey Arnett termed the period from 18–25 years as 'emerging adulthood'. It incorporates the transition from adolescent to adult (school to work/further study), often termed the third transition. Just like the transitions into primary and secondary school, it can be a stressful and difficult time for young people. At this stage, most young people have become closer to maintaining a particular identity, including their role and purpose. Their relationships with the adults around them become more readily based on love and respect as they realise their parents aren't so bad after all.

Young adults tend to be more responsible and plan for a future, but they still need (and are more accepting of) an adult's presence in their life to help them set goals and develop strategies to achieve these. See Chapter 3 for more information on young adults still living at home.

THE TEENAGE BRAIN

We now know a person's brain does not fully develop until they are in their mid-20s. It helps to explain why young adults sometimes make poor decisions and behave in a difficult way.

Their ability to understand and deal with information and conflicting ideas; plan and organise complex events; understand the consequences of their actions; and control their emotions is still under construction. Your older teen may be able to watch multiple screens and listen to music at the same time, but they will have difficulty keeping track of multiple thoughts. They will also struggle to recall past experiences to help make a present decision or prioritise several tasks, which can be frustrating for parents to witness. What to do – check Instagram, wash the dishes, or do the biology assignment that is due first thing in the morning?

Teenagers also tend to still use the primitive part of the brain (known as the amygdala) when they consider the risk associated with different behaviours, which is at odds with their increased physical and social capacity to engage in such behaviours (e.g. sexual activity, drug use). This is why adults are still desperately needed to help set boundaries and limits for their teenagers, most notably when it comes to issues of safety.

A TESTING TIME FOR ALL

In summary, adolescents are faced with four main challenges in making the journey from childhood to adulthood (and a few years after that for some):

- Forming a positive identity
- Establishing a set of good friends
- Breaking the emotional bonds with their adult carers
- Setting meaningful vocational goals

At the same time, adolescence is characterised by:

- a belief in one's immortality
- a desire to experiment
- a need for peer approval
- relatively short-term relationships.

When you look at these two lists together, it's not hard to see why developmental changes in these years can be testing for everyone, especially parents. Our biggest fear is that teenagers engaging in risky behaviours may compromise their health or wellbeing to the extent that it affects outcomes in adulthood. The good news is that parents can use strategies and take actions to help to limit the likelihood of any serious consequences – so read on!

In some cases, parents may need more help than a book can give them. So how do you know when you need professional help with your teenager? Ask yourself these questions:

- Does your child have the capacity to obtain, maintain and retain friendships? This is not necessarily a numbers game – the quality of friendships is more important than how many they have.
- Does your child willingly engage in social situations, such as parties, sleepovers or family gatherings, or do these situations make your child anxious?

- Does your child regularly attend school and engage in school events?
- Does your child have 'islands of competence'? That is, something that your child loves to do that gives them a sense of purpose, such as art or sporting activities.

If the answer to most or all of these questions is no, or the responses have given you reason for concern, speak to your GP. They may recommend making an appointment for you and your child with a psychologist or counsellor to talk about some of these issues and work on strategies to improve your child's wellbeing.

Chapter 3
Why are young adults still at home?

It may seem strange to discuss young adults in a book about parenting teenagers. But the fact is that it's increasingly common for children over the age of 18 to still be living at home. In Australia, according to the ABS, young adults are now more likely to be living with their parents than they were forty years ago, with almost one in three young adults aged 18–34 still living at home compared to one in five in 1976. Over the past forty years, the median ages of marriage for both men and women have risen markedly, and the number of young adults engaged in university or other post-secondary education has almost doubled. There has also been an increase in young people returning to live with their parents after they have spent some time away from home. In fact, the probability that someone will return home at least once before turning 35 is now almost one in two.

What this means is that more and more parents are finding themselves negotiating a new relationship with an adult housemate who once was their dependant child.

The common narrative in Australia today is that parents have failed to provide the right set of circumstances for their young adults to leave home, and are consequently being bled dry by the demands of kids who have never grown up – colloquially termed 'kidults'. But is this fair? It's not uncommon in other countries for young adults to live in the family home until they are married. For example, according to Eurostat, a majority of Italians aged 18–34 still live at home with their parents. There is an expectation that they move from the family home to the married home, even though they may already have full-time jobs – they are not called *mammoni* (Mummies' boys) or *bamboccioni* (big babies) for no reason. In East Asia it is equally common to see children living with parents until they marry or move for employment. Moving out earlier may sometimes seen as a betrayal, that a child is 'fleeing' and abandoning ageing parents.

The transition from adolescent to adult can be stressful and difficult for some young people. In our book *The Princess Bitchface Syndrome 2.0*, we talked about the lack of any formal rites of passage in mainstream Australia that say, 'Now you are an adult'. In some cultures, initiation ceremonies mark the rite of passage from child to adult, such as those held by Aboriginal Australians for children between the ages of 10 to 16 years, or the Jewish tradition of bat mitzvah for girls and bar mitzvah for boys. In parts of Central and South America, there is the *quinceaneras* celebration, which marks a girl's 15th birthday. The celebration recognises the transition to womanhood, and dates back many centuries.

The rapid biological changes of adolescence can result in confusion, uncertainty and 'status anxiety'. More attention needs to be paid to this third transition period (school to work), and what parents and teens need to navigate this critical bridge to adulthood successfully. In Australia, events such as schoolies week at the end of Year 12 seem to have become a default rite of passage. Unfortunately, excessive alcohol and other drug use has often become a major element of the festivities.

WHAT ARE THE REASONS FOR STAYING AT OR MOVING BACK HOME?

There are three main reasons why young adults remain in the parental home:

- They *can't* move: they don't yet have the finances or the means to make the move (e.g. they may be at university, unemployed or underemployed, or dealing with a mental illness or disability)
- They *won't* move: they lounge about and don't seem motivated to do anything (e.g. they may not keep a job for long, may sleep all day, keep different hours), possibly as a result of depression or a sense of entitlement
- They move *back* home: these 'Boomerang kids' may return home after a period of living elsewhere for a range of reasons (e.g. they may want to save money, be unable to get work, or move home because a relationship or move away didn't turn out well)

Here are some more detailed examples.

> Adam was the youngest of three children. He stayed
> in the family home, at the encouragement of his
> parents, in order to concentrate on and finish his
> undergraduate degree. He was keen to save money
> and eventually move into his own apartment closer to
> the city. He was determined to remain positive about
> living with his parents, sharing the load and having an
> adult relationship with them. But the reality turned
> out to be different. His mum gave him a curfew, did
> all his washing and ironing, and was unhappy when
> Adam brought any friends home. Adam felt like he
> was back to being a child again – and things got even
> worse when he found his mum was opening his mail
> and looking through his personal belongings.

Having an adult child at home isn't necessarily a
negative experience, but it's important that some new
rules and expectations are set up so that everyone has the
right to enjoy their own space and time. Negotiate the
terms, expectations and conditions of living with them
as early as possible after they turn 18. Here's a good start
to the conversation: 'You've had eighteen years to figure
out how to make it on your own. Now's the time to put
it into practice.'

There should be two sets of rules – one that reflects
your values and morals (e.g. treat others with respect,
don't abuse alcohol) and one that is about how to live
with each other. What are each person's responsibilities

to keep the house running? How do you stay informed about each other's comings and goings? Is your young adult expected to contact you if they plan to stay out all night? What sort of support are parents expected to offer (e.g. financial support, regular meals)?

> Natasha had finished school at the end of last year, and spent the summer 'recovering' from her exams and the stress of Year 12. But as the year went on, her mother, Barbie, noticed that Natasha wasn't doing anything about starting the next phase of her life. She was rarely in bed before the early hours and didn't get up until the early afternoon, and when she was awake she seemed to watch endless videos and exchange selfies with friends before heading out to clubs in the late evening. Barbie was a single parent, and she'd had enough of supporting Natasha without any recognition. When she confronted Natasha about her plans, Natasha looked her square in the eye and said, 'Mum, mind your own business. I'm an adult now – you can't make me do anything.'

It may be that young adults act out in final years of high school and beyond because of anxiety and/or a fear of future – they have been in the school/home cocoon for eighteen years and the alternative is scary. Playing video games or going out all night and sleeping in, may be driven by fear of moving on. But adult children who refuse to move out or get on with their lives may also have a false sense of entitlement. They may not be willing to start at the bottom of the pack, work or study hard, or link effort to reward.

A survey conducted by budgeting account provider, thinkmoney.co.uk, has revealed that in the UK, nearly half a million young working adults often live a privileged life, with their doting parents still doing their washing, ironing, cooking and cleaning. Some 84 per cent of parents with grown-up children living at home admitted doing laundry for them, while a quarter even tidied their bedrooms. Almost half of the young adults questioned stated that they did no food shopping, and the same proportion paid no rent.

There are times when you may have to enact consequences for unacceptable behaviour. For example, if they don't have a job, encourage them to live as though they do (e.g. on weeknights they have to come home by a certain hour and complete some household chores). Continuing to treat your adult offspring as a child only diminishes their self-esteem and disables them from moving on.

> Sophia's move back home was only a couple of months after her parents' later life divorce, when she was struggling to find work after a period of illness. She moved in with her mother, who was very lost and unhappy. Sophia initially felt like she became a replacement for her father. But soon a rhythm emerged in the household. Sophia cooked meals and cleaned the house in exchange for low rent, which made her feel better about the generous deal.
> Her mother thrived in the company and the novelty

of having Sophia and her friends around. She learnt to use an iPad, on which she joined (and subsequently attended) several MeetUp groups. Within a couple of years, Sophia had found her dream job in a new city and her mother was back on her feet. While Sophia's parting was sad, living at home had made her and her mother's relationship particularly special as a renewed adult relationship.

If your young adult is a boomerang kid, help them set some concrete goals that will ensure they get back on their feet as soon as possible. If they don't meet these goals or fail to make progress where it should be reasonable for them to do so, it may be time to review the arrangement.

The nature of the new relationship may also depend on how much you *like* the company of your adult child, not just how much you love them. It can be nice to have another grown up around to share a glass of wine with, or go to the cinema. But if you don't get along, it can be like living back in the share houses of your university days – tolerating someone you don't get on with.

Should I charge them rent?

Whether you charge rent or not, and how much, will depend on how realistic this is under your child's current circumstances. If you think they still need to learn some lessons about budgeting and being responsible with money, and they have an income, then go for it. Ditto if they are spending their money only on discretionary items, such as going out with friends. But if they understand money and are trying to save for a deposit and you can afford it, think about charging a smaller amount or setting the money aside for a down payment. After all, it will help them to move out more quickly.

The Australian Temperament Project, a study that looked at a group of children over three decades well into adulthood, found that direct financial assistance from parents was still very common for young adults in their early 20s. But most interesting was that around 86 per cent of these young adults felt they could count on their parents to listen to them, help with problems or advise them on other matters, especially if they still lived at home.

Parents play a far more important role in their children's lives in young adulthood than simply providing financial assistance or a place to sleep. It's worth keeping in mind that you still play an important role in your young adult's life, no matter the circumstances.

Part 2

Successfully navigating the teen years

A powerful and useful thing that you can do as a parent to prepare for the teenage years is to arm yourself early with information, knowledge and advice about what to expect. This includes understanding the direct effect that your parenting style, your communication strategies and your willingness to set boundaries and limits have on your teenager's wellbeing.

It may feel a lot like you are becoming unimportant in the teen years, but nothing could be further from the truth. You matter (even if they refuse to let you know it). This section provides the information and tools for creating a home and parenting environment that gives your teenager the best chance of growing into a healthy and happy adult. Dip in, try things out, and come back to learn what works best for your individual child as they continue to grow.

To start on a positive note, while this book largely deals with issues and challenges that will crop up, it's important not to lose track of how to enjoy the teenage years as well. As mentioned in the introduction, teenagers are often talked about in the most negative terms. So here's an exercise to refocus on the positives about your teenager. Ask yourself these questions:

- What did your teenager do or say that made you laugh most recently? Teenagers have a unique world view that can result in some hilarious observations about the quirks of life. Give them the chance to express their views, and tune in.

- What does your teenager have or do that you admire? It may be an activity, such as sporting talent, drama or art, or a characteristic such as kindness towards animals, or the ability to laugh at their own misfortunes.

- Has your teenager said or done something lately that has surprised you (in a positive way)? Occasionally teenagers will act in a way that you weren't expecting. Did your daughter offer her grandfather a drink, or did your son clear the table after dinner? Make a point of observing what they do, and you may be pleasantly surprised at what you find. Then thank them for the action you observed.

- What brings out the best in your teenager? Have you noticed what motivates your teenager to achieve or do well at something? What's the mix of opportunity and support that means they will put in the extra effort?

Paying attention to the positive moments and openly acknowledging them will help to build a relationship with your teenager and increase their self-worth. Remember, part of this is counteracting the messages that tell us looks are the most important thing – it's about finding a thousand ways to say 'You are smart', 'You are funny' or 'You are brave' instead.

Chapter 4
Parenting styles

One of the biggest shocks for parents is the radical (and often lightning fast) change that they have to make to their parenting strategies when the preteen and teenage years arrive. Teenagers are often a contradiction – they still need to feel their parents' strength and love, but their ultimate goal is to achieve freedom, and they seem willing to do all they can to attain it. This results in moments where the same incident, such as offering your teenager a lift to a friend's place, can give rise to different reactions from one day to the next. The first day they will hug you and thank you profusely; the next, they will accuse you of stifling their independence and stomp off to the bus stop, slamming the front door on the way out for effect.

Deep down, teenagers know that they would be well and truly undone if they were too successful at dismantling our authority. The more that young people feel adrift and alone without parental support, the more vulnerable they are to negative outcomes. So effective parenting is about striking a balance between being an army sergeant and Mother Teresa.

PARENTING STYLES

To understand how parenting influences the development of children and teenagers, we need to look at different parenting styles. Every parent has a 'parenting script' that was learned when *they* were raised by their parents, and this often influences how they parent their own children. There are two well-recognised components to this parenting script:

1. **Responsiveness** – this is the extent to which parents intentionally foster their child's individuality and self-management, and support them in meeting their particular demands and needs.
2. **Demandingness** – this is the extent to which, and the methods by which, parents set boundaries and limits, including monitoring and supervision and negotiating a discipline system centred on accountability.

It is the mix of these components that characterise different parenting styles. Research has consistently shown that parenting styles can influence whether an individual has positive or negative outcomes both in adolescence and adulthood. Psychologist Diana Baumrind's work in the 1970s was hugely influential and is still most commonly used in defining these styles. She coined the terms permissive, authoritarian and authoritative to describe different styles, which are explained here.

Authoritarian: command and control

Authoritarian parents are highly demanding and directive, but not responsive. Many authoritarian parents seek to provide a highly ordered and structured environment with clearly stated rules that they expect to be obeyed without explanation. Quiet acceptance of these rules is rewarded – there is little room for negotiation or questioning the rules. Authoritarian parents are also more likely to use punishment to control children's behaviours.

Corporal punishment (e.g. smacking, belting) is often a strategy in authoritarian parenting, as most people labour under the delusion that this produces better behaved kids. In fact, it is hard to ignore the high-quality evidence that links authoritarian parenting to a number of poor outcomes, including antisocial behaviour, aggression, mental illness, low self-esteem and even obesity. Corporal punishment may momentarily control behaviour, but it doesn't help a child learn to self-regulate their behaviours and emotions. This is a significant problem when a UNICEF report released in 2014 indicates that around six out of ten children aged 2–14 are subjected to corporal punishment worldwide. Boys are more likely to experience corporal punishment – and this modelling of physical aggression and control can spill over into the use of violence in adulthood.

Authoritative: limits set, but negotiated

Authoritative parents are both demanding and responsive; in other words, 'firm but fair'. Clear standards and expectations are provided for their child's behaviour, and they are supportive rather than punitive in monitoring these. They want children to be assertive and self-reliant, socially responsible and cooperative. Authoritative parents are likely to offer calm explanations of why limits and boundaries are in place, rather than simply expecting blind adherence to them, but they still communicate that they expect their children to behave appropriately. They:

- say no when it is often easier to say yes
- recognise that children have rights, but with rights come responsibilities
- recognise that they also have rights (e.g. to a peaceful home environment)
- offer empathy, not just sympathy
- notice their child's strengths and comment on them, rather than focusing on weaknesses
- believe in consequential learning from mistakes (where safe)
- expect responsible behaviour.

Authoritative parenting has been associated with positive developmental outcomes for teenagers, such as delayed and reduced alcohol and substance use.

Fred's parents were furious that they had set a curfew but Fred had ignored this and come home half an hour late from a party. He claimed his phone had run out of charge, but when his parents asked why he hadn't borrowed someone else's phone, he just shrugged and said nothing. They lectured him, yelled at him and demanded that he show more respect in future. Fred wasn't given a chance to respond. The following week he was allowed to attend another party and was given the same curfew, but this time he came home forty-five minutes late.

When they came to me for counselling with this issue, I explained to Fred's parents that authoritative parents don't waste their energy yelling and lecturing. I suggested that they skip the long lecture, as the evidence shows this approach doesn't work. Instead I taught them the two most impactful methods that authoritative parents use when their offspring break curfew.

1. **Briefly decrease the curfew time.** Since Fred had arrived home twenty minutes late and made no phone call, authoritative parents would respond by calmly informing Fred that his curfew would be twenty minutes earlier for the following week. Authoritative parents remind Fred of the consequence of not being home on time. When Fred demonstrates that he is

capable of complying with the curfew for a week, he can resume his normal curfew time.

2. **Generate supplementary boundaries.** If Fred were to return home more than an hour late, or is a multiple offender and breaks curfew more than once, authoritative parents will often create an additional consequence to help him realise the magnitude of his mistake. Preventing him from socialising with his mates or removing wi-fi access for a specific period of time can drive the point home. Authoritarian parents eschew lengthy punishments, as restricting phone or internet use for weeks on end will demotivate, discourage and dishearten Fred and may incite even worse behaviour.

PERMISSIVE/INDULGENT: NO LIMITS OR BOUNDARIES

These parents are more responsive than demanding. They are laidback and easygoing, and do not expect mature behaviour but instead assume that their teenager has the maturity to act in their own best interests. They avoid confrontation and conflict, shying away from any decision making or actions that make them feel negative emotions or discomfort.

A permissive parent may feel that they are conscientious, engaged and committed to their teenager, but this is often characterised by wanting to be their child's best friend rather than their parent. And while all children need to feel connected to and loved by their parents, they also need a regular dose of Vitamin 'N' (for no), something the permissive parent is reluctant to employ.

One of the most extreme examples of permissive parenting outlined in *The Prince Boofhead Syndrome* was that of Texas teenager Ethan Couch. Newspapers reported that in June 2013, at the tender age of 16, Couch was caught on video stealing two cases of beer from a Walmart store and driving with seven passengers in his father's pick-up truck. Couch, who was drunk, illegally driving on a restricted licence and speeding, lost control and hit four people on the side of the road, killing them instantly, and injuring many of those in the truck.

A psychologist hired by Couch's defence team claimed that Ethan needed rehabilitation instead of prison, that he was so extremely wealthy and spoiled that he could not tell right from wrong. The psychologist claimed that the way that Couch had been parented 'strongly enabled' the deadly accident, despite the fact that Couch's blood alcohol level was three times the legal limit.

One article suggested that Couch was parented without reasonable boundaries, and that he was taught that other people were beneath him and less worthy than him. A witness for the defence claimed the teenager was a product of 'profoundly dysfunctional parents' who never taught him the consequences of his actions. His parents had each had their own brushes with the law, and at one point his mother even fled to Mexico with him.

Thankfully, extreme cases such as this are rare. But it's a good example of how giving a child everything and imposing zero consequences can go disastrously wrong.

Uninvolved/neglectful parenting

In the 1980s a fourth parenting style was added to Baumrind's three – uninvolved or neglectful parenting. This is when parents are neither responsive nor demanding. They believe that their job is to provide necessities only (e.g. food, shelter, etc.) without any emotional input. Uninvolved parenting styles can be damaging, but be aware that they may also be a consequence of factors impacting the ability of a parent to do their best job, such as mental illness or substance misuse.

WHAT IS THE BEST PARENTING STYLE?

Research suggests that in Western society, authoritative parenting is most likely to be associated with positive outcomes in later life. Of course, no parent exclusively uses one style or the other – we usually employ a mix of approaches depending on the age of our children, our family circumstances and the nature of the decisions to be made at any one time. There are also cultural differences; for example, a 2009 study from the Universidad de Valencia, Spain, of over 1400 Spanish teenagers showed that the optimal parenting style was permissive, explained as the cultural acceptance of affection, reasoning and involvement without strictness.

However, I include information on the different styles to encourage you to think about your overall approach to parenting, the strategies that have been inherited as a result of your own experiences of parenting, and how they may contribute to conflict with your teenager.

Here are a couple of examples of when parenting

strategies seem helpful, but can lead to unintended consequences.

I'm their best friend!

Parents often tell me that they don't like to be strict with their children, particularly girls, because they had strict parents and hated it. You may find it hard to believe, but your teenager may feel resentful towards you in the long term for not setting limits and taking more control, as they will not have had the opportunity to build the resilience they need to cope in the adult world.

I find it difficult to understand or sympathise with the 'I am my daughter's best friend' brigade. This is mainly because it is carved into a teenage girl's DNA to test the rules at some stage. The appropriate response from a parent is to uphold the rules (or calmly renegotiate them if necessary). Once you identify as a friend and stop setting boundaries for your daughter, it becomes monumentally difficult to rein things back in. How confusing will it be to your child if you fluctuate between best friend and parent? Leave her friends to be her friends and step up to be her parent instead. Besides, show me a 14-year-old who wants a 45-year-old best friend!

They need help with their science project!

Almost everyone is acquainted with the parent who 'rescued' their child from poor time management to complete a project or submit a book review. Lately, these 'helicopter' parents have been starting to morph into 'snowplough' parents, trying to remove all obstacles for their child. They're the ones ringing academic staff to complain about their son's mid-semester marks (then making calls to the department chair and the academic dean!), or accompanying their young adult daughter to job interviews and asking to sit in.

A growing number of parents are reluctant to cut the psychological and emotional apron strings, denying their teenagers the opportunity to gain their own levels of proficiency, satisfaction and wellbeing. Instead they leave behind anxious children who are ill equipped to deal with matters themselves, whether small or large. Children need to face and overcome obstacles so that they can learn to trust themselves to make good decisions in the face of adversity, and to build resilience when things don't work out as planned.

It's dangerous out there!

Despite the rarity of violent crimes against strangers, many children live highly orchestrated lives. They are driven to school and social events, and their mobile phones become the world's longest umbilical cords, attaching them to anxious parents, who text them frequently to 'see how they are going'.

Yet raising resilient children means providing them with opportunities that will help them manage risk and overcome setbacks, which can't occur if they are raised in a parent-reinforced bubble. How do kids learn to ride a bike? They fall off. How do kids learn to deal with pain? By being hurt. How do kids learn to assess risk? By being exposed to danger. This must intuitively make sense to parents, but many are nevertheless hamstrung by their own fear of pain, risk and danger, and simply cannot tolerate the idea of their children experiencing these.

As a psychologist, my role is to help parents understand how their unconscious drives and motivations play out in their relationships with their children. Trying to control a teenager's environment all the time naturally triggers a teen's defensiveness, which not only shuts down communication but often results in more frequent attempts to defy any boundaries that are set in the first instance. It's really emancipation on steroids – the teenager just ends up pushing harder to separate from family, the emotional temperature shoots through the roof, and anger becomes the language of the relationship.

Teenagers need time and space to explore, assess the intention of strangers, lose their mobile phone (almost inevitably) and still survive. If we fail to offer these opportunities in a developmentally appropriate way, we effectively say to them that we don't have confidence in their ability to look after themselves. The result is that they will feel helpless rather than cared for. As a consequence, they may escape via cyberspace, which is comparatively unsupervised. While they may not be allowed to catch a bus to a friend's place, they can communicate with the entire world from the 'safety' of their own home. A more rational approach seems to be in order.

Chapter 5
Communicating with your teenager

In 2008, Australian country singer Peter Denahy released a popular music video for his hit 'Sort of Dunno Nothin Teenage Song', which is available on YouTube if you'd like a good laugh. Denahy sits at the breakfast table across from a teenage boy, asking the sort of questions familiar to parents everywhere. The answers the teenage boy provides will also be familiar to parents everywhere. The exchange goes something like this (not the actual lyrics, but you get the gist):

How was school?
Good.
Did you have a good day?
Yep.
Are you seeing your friends today?
Yep.
What are you going to get up to?
Nothing.
Where are you meeting?

Dunno.
Who will be there?
Dunno.
Sounds like great fun.
Yep.

The music video is as much about teenage mono-syllable communication as a lack of imagination among adults when it comes to sparking conversation with the younger generation.

To have a proper conversation with a teenager, you must observe the following golden rules:

1. **Disconnect.** Both of you have to disengage from technology to achieve any worthwhile dialogue. This means unplugging from the iThis and iThat, discarding, muting or turning off the mobile, and turning off the TV. No significant or remarkable exchange can take place when one or both parties are distracted by a screen.

2. **Location.** Think about the physical location in which you are attempting to engage with your teenager. Restaurants and cafes can be good if everyone is technology-free, or in the garden or by the pool. Some teens will think best when they are active and mobile, so ditch the intense conversation across the dinner table and go to the park to kick a ball. A drive in the car is also a good strategy; your child is captive and no-one has to make uncomfortable eye contact.

3. **Mood.** Only have the conversation when you are both in the right frame of mind. Solutions to problems are unlikely to be found if one or both of you are angry, exhausted or frustrated. Wait until each party is in a more calm and agreeable state of mind. Express your feelings ('I'm too exhausted to have this conversation right now, let's leave it and make another time') and acknowledge your teen's feelings ('Let me make sure I understand. You're saying you feel . . .').

4. **Clarity.** Make sure you are strong and clear in what you are stating or what information you are seeking. Try not to sugar-coat what you are saying: get straight to the point. Because of their still-developing brains, a teen's attention span is not long. So get to your point quickly, repeat it, use concrete images and pay attention to anything they say.

5. **Culture.** Become a student of teen culture. Enter your teenager's own world and be familiar with what is important to them. Play with social media, watch popular teen shows or movies, and read articles about the latest video games and apps. This isn't an exercise in trying to inhabit your teenager's world – nothing will stop a conversation more quickly than if you try to use the latest lingo. It's an exercise in sharing a common understanding and taking an interest in what is important to them.

Other specific tips for while you are having the conversation:

1. **Choose your battles.** I can't emphasise this enough. It's the single most useful and actionable piece of advice you will find about communicating with teenagers. Don't argue over trivial matters – no-one has ever died of an untidy bedroom. Save your energy for matters related to safety and respect.

2. **Model active listening.** Make sure you are doing less talking and more listening. A common complaint from young people is that their parents don't give them a fair hearing.

3. **Be supportive.** Be your teenager's biggest fan. Give positive feedback when it is deserved. Try to catch your adolescent doing something good, and send a positive message – make it a goal to say at least one positive thing a day. They may do little more than grunt, shrug and slope off to their room, but it's all about putting a penny in the goodwill bank for later on.

4. **Make it clear it's not a competition.** When it gets too heated or is not constructive, stop the conversation – but allow them to have the last word.

5. **Use humour.** Appropriately, that is. Avoid sarcasm and teasing, which can trigger a defensive response and shut the communications door you are trying to open. Laughing together, however, can defuse tension.

6. **Avoid trying to control the situation.** Ultimatums will rarely work – they trigger your teenager's inherent sensitivity to control.

Negotiate, negotiate and then negotiate some more. The trick is to aim for a compromise where everyone wins.

7. **Address the problem and not the person.** Try 'Your lack of respect for your grandfather today was not okay', then give a clear and specific example of what was not acceptable and how to do it differently, rather than saying something like, 'You're such a brat!'

8. **Give your teenager the impression that both parents are on the same page.** If you're not, save the debate for when you and the other parent are alone. United you stand; divided, you are cactus.

9. **Don't constantly remind them of past mistakes.** Adolescence is a time of trial and error. Mistakes are common and expected. Constantly reminding your teenager (with evident relish) about past mistakes makes it less likely they will tell you if they mess up again.

10. **Let some things go by.** One of the most annoying things that parents do is comment on everything their teenager says or does. Parents who engage in a running commentary substantially reduce the likelihood of receiving any information in the future. Imaging how irritating it would be if you had someone constantly commenting on your every action. Surprise! It feels the same to your teenager.

There are two other things to bear in mind that can be frustrating for parents unless you maintain a developmental perspective.

You may think that you've had a constructive conversation about a behaviour, boundary or limit that was clear to everyone at the time, only to have your teenager repeat the same action that prompted the conversation. It's quite possible they have forgotten the conversation or weren't listening as closely as you thought, as their brain is busily processing a vast amount of information at this stage of life. The answer? When a decision is made that you want your teenager to remember, write it down, date it and put it in a spot that you can refer back to if the problem arises again.

Similarly, your teenager may tell you that you said something or communicated a decision (usually in their favour!) that you firmly believe you didn't. Sometimes there is a genuine misalignment with what you actually said and what they wanted to hear, which then becomes the 'truth' to them. Once again, this is common in adolescence when the brain is developing. You may need to stay calm, revisit the conversation or start again and renegotiate the limits or boundaries. Then write it down as above.

Chapter 6
Helping your teenager flourish

Talk to many parents across Australia about what they want for their teenagers, and the word 'happy' often appears alongside other aspirations. Precisely what makes human beings happy has now been studied for almost two decades by a group of psychologists who have decided to call themselves positive psychologists. In positive psychology, flourishing is 'to live within an optimal range of human functioning, one that connotes goodness, generativity, growth, and resilience'. So in essence, flourishing is the other side of depression and lethargy, or living a life where you have a negative view of yourself, your environment and the future.

The following are five key factors that allow young people to flourish.

1. HAVING AN ADULT MENTOR OR ROLE MODEL IN THEIR LIVES

One of the best forms of insurance for the physical and emotional wellbeing of young people is for them to have at least one special adult in their lives. This is the person from whom they can draw strength and who makes them feel safe, valued and listened to. If young people have a special bond that they value highly, they are more likely to think twice before doing anything to damage that connection. Building this connectedness with your adolescent maximises your chance of successful parenting.

In their well-known 2008 article on the mindset of teachers who successfully foster resilience in their students, psychologists Robert Brooks and Sam Goldstein call this the need for a 'charismatic adult' in the life of a young person. They cite Julius Segal, a psychologist and author, who defined a charismatic adult as a person with whom you can identify and from whom you can gather strength. Segal also observed that in a surprising number of cases this person was a teacher. Having someone like this in your child's life can mean the difference between a resilient child who succeeds in spite of adversity and a non-resilient child who does not.

2. HAVING SOMETHING THEY ARE GOOD AT

One of the most important tasks for an early adolescent is the process of developing areas of growing skill and competence. Providing young people with a succession of structured activities they are good at and enjoy (e.g. art, music, sport, dance and drama) and for which they receive recognition is very valuable. It allows them to take healthy risks and mix with peers who share similar interests or values, exposes them to good adult role models, and offers routine among the usual chaos of teenage life. These are often referred to as 'islands of competence' and are helpful in building young people's self-belief.

Meeting one of the key developmental tasks – identity formation – comes from having a go at something and developing a level of proficiency, while learning the importance of practice, persistence and making the connection between effort and outcome. Adult carers need to keep prompting young people not to give up; to persevere even when it's hard. The importance of this cannot be underestimated. Developing a teenager's feelings of competence and confidence will help protect them against the inevitable peer pressures and risk-taking behaviours that can escalate in mid-adolescence. Absorbing the fact that one can obtain success and satisfaction through perseverance will become part of their attitude over time and can build their capacity to face and overcome adversity in the future.

3. HAVING EMOTIONAL INTELLIGENCE

Another crucial advantage in navigating adolescence is the ability to read social situations: to name and recognise the thoughts and emotions of others, and to interpret how other people perceive you. Emotional intelligence is often referred to as EQ. Just as a high IQ can foretell high scores in academic tasks, an elevated EQ can forecast success in social and emotional situations. Think of it as being 'people smart'.

EQ is instrumental in young people being able to establish solid, long-lasting peer relations; increases their ability to solve problems and resolve conflicts; and helps them manage anger and make good decisions. Research indicates that EQ can play an equally important role as IQ in workplace success, especially in maintaining good working relationships. Some people have innately superb EQ, while others need to develop these skills. The good news is that everyone can get better. These skills can be taught, or learned by example.

4. HAVING A SENSE OF MEANING IN THEIR LIVES

It is important for young people to feel connected to something or someone that transcends the material world in which we live. Spirituality (which is broader than but can include being religious) has been identified as a protective factor in adolescence. It is about understanding that your role in life has more value than what you do on a day-to-day basis. Young people who have meaning and purpose in their lives report feeling happier, have a greater sense of control, derive more satisfaction out of life, and experience less stress, anxiety and depression.

How a young person finds this meaning will vary. For some it is related to their own or their family's religious beliefs; for others it is being part of a family, school, team or group, or sometimes volunteering for a cause that they believe makes a difference. The responses will differ for each young person but they all include being part of something bigger than themselves.

5. POSITIVE SELF-TALK AND A WILLINGNESS TO PERSEVERE

Self-talk can be described as our thoughts making themselves known to us, and it influences our self-esteem and confidence, positively or negatively. Each person has several thousand conscious and unconscious thoughts per day that contribute to this. What we think affects how we feel.

Young people can have different thoughts about the same thing. For example, imagine that your teenager is out for a walk and they see a dog. If they think the dog is cute, they will feel calm. However, if they think the dog will bite, they will feel scared. Similarly, if young people tell themselves they are a failure, they will be. If they tell themselves they can succeed, they have a much better chance of doing so. Resilient teenagers talk encouragingly to themselves, and it's important that we reinforce this with positive messages.

A NOTE FOR FATHERS

Having spent years talking to young people about their parents, it's obvious to me that young people, especially boys, get a lot out of being around their fathers: something special and complementary to what their mothers give them.

Children have different relationships with their fathers compared to their mothers, and these relationships are important for their wellbeing. Fathers play a critical, independent role in child development, tend to engage in more physical 'roughhouse' play and are also more likely to encourage children to take risks and embrace challenges. They also model masculinity and manhood, which is incredibly important in a world that is becoming more conscious of gender roles and relations and their effect on wellbeing for both men and women.

Good fathering is not about being seen as a walking wallet; rather, it is about spending quality time with your kids, especially in early adolescence. Sadly, many fathers who work full-time end up spending limited time with their children, the justification being that they are busy providing for the family, by working to pay for a nice house and a good school. However, this is often not in the child's best interests.

Talking and listening, the basics for engaging in and communicating with teenage children, tend to occur while participating in other activities, with trust and self-disclosure growing gradually as a result. Boys tend to open up more while participating in an activity. So doing things together is vital – it allows closeness and for conversation to wander into deeper realms. See if you can find common interests (e.g. a sport, type of art or a board game). Be responsible for taking children to sports or music lessons and get involved – most organisations that run children's activities are crying out for volunteers, and it's a terrific way to be a role model for your kids.

Chapter 7
Making decisions with your teenager

It's hard to make a judgement about when teenagers are ready for different things, and factors such as height, physical maturity or chronological age are not always a reliable guide. But adolescents – depending on personality, temperament and past behaviour – do need to be given developmentally appropriate opportunities for freedom, safe risk-taking, making good decisions and problem solving. After all, they will need these skills to survive in the world as adults.

You'll often get the classic 'But Sophie/Tom/Helena/Rory's parents let them/don't make them do that!' But what another family does is not always a good guide to what will work for your child. Say, 'It's interesting to hear how others deal with these situations. In our house, these are our roles.' Then explain your reasons to your child and try to come up with compromises where both parties are satisfied.

Here is a guide to some common conundrums when parenting adolescents.

IS MY TEENAGER READY TO ... CATCH PUBLIC TRANSPORT ALONE?

The start of secondary school may prompt the decision to allow your child to catch public transport alone. This is often a pragmatic decision as secondary schools may be further away than primary school, and it's more likely that both parents work when children are older.

A story that captured the pros and cons of catching transport alone was that of Lenore Skenazy, a parent who sparked a frenzy when the media found out she had allowed her 9-year-old son to find his own way home from Bloomingdales, a popular department store in New York. The trip included catching the subway alone. Opinions were split, with extreme views on whether this constituted child abuse or whether it's something that all parents should be doing.

The debate around Skenazy was carried out largely by people who did not know the child, his psychology (e.g. temperament and personality) or upbringing and, therefore, were unqualified to offer an opinion. Preparing young people to manage the realities of being out in public involves knowing the unique psychology of your child and role-playing situations at home. For example:

- teaching them to yell, 'Go away, I don't know you!' so that nearby people are alerted to the situation
- knowing the location of safe houses
- practising writing down the number plate of a car or taking a photo with their mobile phone
- avoiding walking in isolated areas.

The most recent statistics from the Australian Institute of Criminology state that just over 750 abductions occurred in Australia during one calendar year and that just over half were by a stranger. Children made up less than 20 per cent of the victims in these cases and many of these child abductions were associated with custody battles.

Most schools now run programs on personal safety, and the family of murdered Queensland teenager Daniel Morcombe has released a number of resources on the Daniel Morcombe Foundation website, including an updated child-safety video tackling bullying and cyber safety, and the Keeping Kids Safe Resources (see www. recognisereactreport.com.au).

IS MY TEENAGER READY TO . . . GET A MOBILE PHONE?

Whether or not to give teenagers a mobile (particularly a smartphone) is first and foremost a parental decision, not that of their peers, school or telecommunication organisations.

Age certainly does not define maturity, but what does help with this decision is your child's history of being able to follow rules at home and at school, and take care of their belongings. Have they shown a reasonable level of responsibility when it comes to observing curfews, notifying you of their whereabouts, looking after younger siblings, regularly fulfilling allocated domestic duties, caring for pets and not losing possessions or money? These questions are important as past behaviour often predicts future behaviour, so if parents detect a sustained pattern of accountability, a sense of duty and fiscal restraint, then the decision to allow a teen to have a smartphone becomes easier.

Specific questions to think about in terms of phone use include the type of phone and the type of plan the child needs. Will they be making lots of calls? Are they on social media (apps such as Instagram that have video content will make large dents in data allowances), or do you ask that they only use social media at home on wi-fi? A cheaper prepaid option may work, where your child will simply run out of credit rather than rack up enormous bills. Do they need a smartphone at all, or will an old-school, basic 'dumb phone' do the job?

A smartphone is not just an expensive piece of technology but a sophisticated communication device and a powerful media-production tool. Teenagers can create memes, images or videos that can be widely distributed and uploaded to websites instantaneously throughout the world. This is why parents should carefully consider if their offspring has the maturity to manage a digital footprint.

If your teenager ticks all the boxes, then draw up a contract that stipulates the rules for phone use, insist that they have obtained the eSmart digital licence (www.digitallicence.com.au) and then monitor and supervise their use.

IS MY TEENAGER READY TO . . . GO TO AN EVENING PARTY?

It is a growing trend for kids in early secondary school to be allowed to have evening parties that finish as late as 10–11 p.m. If the newspapers are to be believed, some teenage parties end with hordes of drunk and drug-affected teens vandalising cars, smashing letterboxes and hurling missiles at police. But the truth is that social gatherings, if handled well, are an important part of tackling key developmental tasks – making new friends and developing social skills, independence and confidence – and can be a valuable learning experience. It is also a good way for parents to meet their offspring's social group. There's no one right way to handle parties, but if events are well planned and the lines of communication are kept open, you can help your child stay safe – and have an enjoyable time.

The police in most states and territories have a party safe kit that parents can use as a guideline (google 'police party safe kit' and your state or territory). If your child is willing to abide by the rules and follow the police guidelines, then parties can be wonderful and memorable milestones in their journey to adulthood. If, on the other hand, your early adolescent wants to attend a party being hosted by someone else, you have to weigh up your child's desire to have fun with your concerns about their safety, especially if the host is someone you do not know.

Parents who come to see me who are concerned about their child attending a party are advised to say, 'I'm worried that you might be in danger at this party. I can't let you go if I'm not sure you'll be safe.' If you already know your child's friends and their parents, it can be easier to agree to your child attending the event. If you are acquainted with the host parents and know they share similar values to you, this may give you confidence that your child will be properly supervised. It's imperative that you find out who is hosting the party and contact them to ascertain:

- whether or not there will be adult supervision, including some form of security
- how many people will be there
- if there will be alcohol present
- what time it starts and finishes
- if the party will stay in one place or move somewhere else during the night.

If your teen refuses to share the location and contact details of the host party, then it is quite reasonable for you to say no.

Your safety concerns are likely to diminish over time, as your teen becomes wiser and you get to know their friends. You may also discover that as they mature they will come up with strategies for dealing with safety concerns themselves.

IS MY TEENAGER READY TO ... STAY AT HOME ALONE ALL DAY?

The school holidays are approaching, and your teen is begging you to not send them to the council holiday program. After all, they insist, they're old enough to look after themselves!

Is your child old enough to be left home alone? You may feel under some pressure because the amount of annual leave at your workplace nowhere near matches the number of weeks that school holidays seem to endlessly go on for.

Peer pressure may be part of the decision too, both for your teenager and for you. No doubt your child will put forth an argument that 'Jordan's parents let him stay alone all the time!' You may be chatting to other parents and realise that it's becoming more common for them to leave their teenage children to look after themselves for a day. It may be a standard arrangement in some families from different cultures, and for some families, it may be the only choice financially.

Calls to kids' and parent helplines indicate that some teenagers can feel anxious and lonely, and parents filled with worry and guilt, if the move is made too soon. There's no right answer because children mature at different rates. You may have a 13-year-old who you feel completely confident can stay at home alone safely, or you may have a 16-year-old who you're still not sure you can trust to keep the pet rabbit alive for more than a day.

Laws require parents to be responsible for their children and to make reasonable decisions about their safety at all times. In Australia there is no overarching law that states an age by which parents may or may not leave their child home alone. Laws vary across states and territories; for example, in Queensland, if a child under 12 years of age is left alone for an 'unreasonable time' without observation, police can charge adult carers with having committed a misdemeanour. However, the rule also says that whether the time is unreasonable is contingent on all the relevant circumstances. Elsewhere in Australia, the law says you're legally obliged to make sure that your child is properly cared for by providing food, clothing, a place to live, safety and supervision. If your child is left in a hazardous situation, not adequately fed, clothed or provided with proper shelter, you could be charged with wrongdoing. The authorities, be it the police or child protection services, have the right to remove children from circumstances where they deem the child's safety is at risk and where there's no adult present.

What all this means is that you need to use your own judgement about leaving children home alone. Think about whether your child can cope if you aren't able to get back, or if something happens beyond the wi-fi failing. It should be a decision that everyone is comfortable with, so consider whether they seem anxious or comfortable during the discussion. Have a safety plan in place that includes family and friends, as well as emergency phone numbers. Include some landline numbers where possible, in case mobile networks are disrupted. A back-up childcare option may also be useful.

Here are some questions to ask before you make the decision with your child:

- Can you try short periods at home alone first, to see how it goes? How did everyone feel about it? Do you need to review plans/rules?
- Who can they call on if they need something? Neighbours? Friends? Do they know emergency phone numbers?

- Who can take your child for the remainder of the day if they are not comfortable with being home alone? Can you come home if needed?
- What are the rules about answering the phone, answering the doorbell, using technology (e.g. how many hours, can they use social media?) or using the oven/heater/washing machine/dryer? Don't assume they know the rules for these things. Have your teenager repeat the rules back to you to make sure you have a common understanding.
- How are they expected to help around the house if they are home with time to spare? Is there homework that needs to be completed?
- Are friends allowed over? Who and how many? Do their parents know that there isn't an adult at home?
- Can they leave home and go to a friend's house? Whose house? Is an adult present there? How do they get there and back?
- If they are moving around during the day, what are the rules about letting you know? Have them tell you their plan for the day, and encourage them to let you know if it changes.

Some other things to discuss include making sure your child knows when you will be back, and arranging to call at set times to see how they are going. Don't let that stop you from also making calls at times that will be less expected by your teen. Consider how well siblings are likely to get along, especially if they are to be left together for a long period of time. Consider what is available in the house (e.g. medication and alcohol) and decide the extent to which you need to keep those things out of reach.

Discuss with your teen what they would do in an emergency (e.g. what if a fire started or someone was trying to break in? What if their sibling had an asthma attack?). In the end, only you and your teenager can weigh up the pros and cons of them staying home alone and make a decision. If the time doesn't feel right but you still need to be away from home, you might try to enlist the help of family or friends. You might swap some days of care with families of your teenager's friends, juggle holidays with partners or other single parents, or use teenage holiday programs run by local councils, until you both feel confident with any plans.

SHOULD MY TEENAGER . . . HAVE A CURFEW?

There's a lot to consider here. Many experts recommend curfews because they set clear boundaries for your teen. Make sure your expectations are realistic and based on the specific event they are attending. Be rational. There's no universal requirement for when teenagers should be home, but the American Academy of Pediatrics recommends that 12–13-year-olds are home no later than 8 p.m. on weeknights and 10 p.m. on the weekend, and 14–16-year-olds are home no later than 9 p.m. on weeknights and 11 p.m. on weekends.

Ultimately this is your decision and should be based on your assessment of your child's personality, temperament and past behaviour. Involving them in the discussion means they are more likely to cooperate and adhere to the schedule. All rules must have consequences (see page 75), but it's also a good move to reward them for compliance.

There are also times that they *want* you to say no.

> It was the end of the school year and Daisy's friends were planning a huge sleepover party to finish up Year 8. The plan became more elaborate as the day went on – in the end there were four boys and three girls planning to catch the train to Kai's beach house. A couple of the boys had become drunk at a party last month and had been thrown out, and they'd also been in trouble with the police after being caught writing graffiti on the local shopping centre walls. Daisy was tired from the school year and a little anxious about the talk going on. She was relieved when she ran the idea past her mum and the answer was a firm 'no'. She returned to school the next day, complaining about how inflexible and mean her mum was, but she couldn't help feeling relieved.

If your child is under peer pressure to attend or do something that they don't feel ready for or are anxious about, it makes it much easier if they can blame their parents for not being allowed to participate.

Chapter 8
Setting rules and limits

One of the keys to parenting adolescents is making sure they feel (and are) safe. This can be communicated by establishing, early in adolescence, a set of rules that are negotiated and agreed on by both sides. The smart money is on parents who create a negotiated system of rewards and punishments that lets adolescents feel that they have some ownership of the rules rather than having to simply obey the ones their parents chose.

Be sure to set clear boundaries, as doing so communicates to your offspring that you care. Boundaries and explicit guidelines help your teenager to remain safe while they are still a 'work in progress'. Many parents are hesitant to set limits, which can create the likes of Prince Boofheads and Princess Bitchfaces who feel entitled to do whatever they like.

A word of caution, though. If your teenager feels *too* constrained by rules and limits, it's likely to have the opposite effect and result in classic scenes of teenage rebellion and titanic power struggles. Consider this example.

Robyn felt like she was giving her 15-year-old daughter, Milla, very clear guidance about rules and expectations, which was exactly what all the parenting experts recommended.

Milla was expected to complete her homework and chores before she was free to do what she wished on the weekends. Technology was not to be used between 10 a.m. and 6 p.m. If she went out, Robyn expected to know where and when, who Milla would be with and what they were doing. Robyn also used multiple apps on her own and Milla's phones to track Milla's movements and to make sure she was where she said she would be, and she had all of Milla's social media passwords to check what she was doing with her friends online.

With all this effort, Robyn was shocked when she had to contact Milla late one night about a family emergency. After ringing Milla's phone multiple times, Milla's friend's mother answered the phone. Milla and a group of boys and girls had been out since mid-afternoon but she wasn't sure where. Milla must have accidently left her phone at the house. Robyn was furious – the minute Milla walked in the door, she was going to be grounded for a month.

Robyn has set herself up for an A-grade power struggle with her 15-year-old daughter, who has been resourceful enough to find a way around her mother's efforts at control. Instead of flying off the handle when Milla comes home, Robyn would do well to engage in a constructive conversation with Milla about how both their needs can be met in such a way that Robyn feels comfortable with Milla's safety and wellbeing, and Milla feels like she has some autonomy.

Sometimes we need to invest a little trust in our teenagers and give them the opportunity to do the right thing.

CONSEQUENCES

When the rules have been negotiated, and things still go wrong, many parents report that nothing they do seems to work.

Try thinking of privileges as a motivator for your teen. Removing or permitting a privilege should ideally provide an incentive for a young person to make better choices that are more in line with your values, attitudes and beliefs – the rules of your house. The most potent consequence is limiting access to something your child wants and enjoys. This may be video or computer games, mobile phone use, social media, peer contact, driving a car, or spending time on a loved hobby. In the example just given, Milla needs to experience some consequences for breaking her mother's trust, but grounding Milla for a month may be hard to stick to and could be counterproductive. Examples of more appropriate consequences might be:

- no phone or internet use for two days – if it happens again, four days, and so on
- having to cook a meal every night for a week and wash the dishes.

You have to be the world expert on your child in order to choose the right privilege to revoke as a consequence. Who are their friends? What do they like doing? What would it really annoy them to lose for a short period of time?

You also need to have the intestinal fortitude to stick to your guns and withhold that privilege until the time you stipulated has expired. Giving in only teaches them that you are all hot air and bluster and they will simply never take you seriously.

But what if your consequences don't seem to work? There are two areas to examine. The first is to ask what lies behind the child's pattern of bad choices – is there a need that is not being met? The other is to examine the length of time consequences are being imposed. Is it too short, so that your child doesn't really care? Is it too long, meaning that your child can't possibly be successful (e.g. no swearing for a whole month)?

Many people who come to see me want their teenager's behaviour to change instantly. This is not a realistic goal, but encouraging them to practise and develop improved decision making is. If you expect flawless behaviour immediately, you will be disappointed. Like any new skill, making better choices takes practice.

When instigating a new regime, you must expect the odd setback. At the start, many parents tell me that their teenager makes poor choices on a daily basis and experiences the consequences often. Rather than throwing in the towel and giving up or deciding that you've chosen the wrong consequence, be patient. All young people require time to practise different choices. And they need their parents' iron resolve to keep them practising.

WHAT TO DO WHEN YOU'RE DESPERATE

Sabine was at her wits' end. Both she and her husband had tried everything – threats, rewards, punishment, yelling, incentives – but their three teenage sons continued to be chronically slothful. Sabine could not stand another day of coming home from work only to have to navigate her way through a sea of dirty sports clothes, football boots, fast-food wrappers and school textbooks simply to get from the front door to the kitchen. Especially since, on the way through, she would inevitably see one or more of her sons lying on the couch or the floor watching Netflix with multiple friends and girlfriends.

Desperate times can call for desperate measures. I suggest a family meeting where the parents propose a new protocol (no more raised voices) and a straightforward plan whereby any belongings left in the public areas of the house will simply be placed in the deep freezer in the garage. There will be nothing said: that's where their things will be. After a few weeks of frozen socks and undies, the message will be well and truly received.

GIVE THEM YOUR TRUST AND RESPECT

The best relationships between teenagers and their parents are based on trust and respect. But many parents instead find themselves floundering in a sea of desperation and anxiety. Ideally, trust and respect grow incrementally as rules and regulations are negotiated. In this way, the young person comes to associate compliance with the possibility of having rules renegotiated in their favour if they demonstrate their trustworthiness.

If parents are consistent and follow through with limits and consequences, the young person will usually respond in kind. If, on the other hand, you change the rules and fail to keep promises, your teenager will run like a Sherman tank through the framework you have attempted to set up.

Chapter 9
Strengthening families

It is entirely developmentally normal for teenagers to prefer to be with their mates over hanging out with their parents. A sense of belonging and connectedness to a peer group is a powerful protective factor for wellbeing in adolescence and beyond. But peer friendships and relationships do not replace the ongoing importance of family connectedness and belonging (no matter how much your teenager tries to convince you otherwise). People who feel like outsiders in their family, peer group or community tend to be more at risk of mental illness than those with strong bonds. Close knit families are built around shared positive experiences, plenty of positive communication and family rituals or traditions.

There will always be opportunities for you to spend time with your teenager, and it's important to take these when they arise. You may want to schedule some activities in, especially (but not exclusively) over the holidays when everyone is more relaxed and with a bit more time up their sleeves. But always be looking for opportunities;

for example, if your teenager's plans fall through on a Saturday, seize the day!

Research shows that, generally speaking, the sheer amount of time parents spend with younger children has little effect on outcomes including academic achievement and emotional wellbeing. Instead, *quality* time is the key, when we are focused and engaged with our full attention on our children. This includes reading to children, sharing a meal and talking to them without being interrupted by phones, social media or other demands.

A longitudinal study in the US, published in the *Journal of Marriage and Family* in 2015 found that quantity alongside quality of time does, however, start to become more important in the teenage years. Time spent with mothers reduced the likelihood of delinquent behaviour, and time with both parents together, such as at meal times, reduced the likelihood of substance abuse. These positive associations were found with teenagers who spent an average of six hours per week engaged in family time – so we're not talking huge amounts of time here. You can't necessarily mark the hour at which you will engage in quality time on a daily basis with your children, but you can create spaces where it is more likely to happen. There's no recommendations about specific amount of quality time that should be spent with children, but what appears to be important is that parents are not stressed, anxious or sleep deprived during this time.

Whatever activity you share, it's also important that your child enjoys it. It's tempting to use the time to catch up on watching your favourite David Attenborough docos or have your teen help rearrange the bookshelf, but engaging them in activities of your choice is counterproductive and reduces the likelihood that the opportunity will arise again. Let them help decide on the activity. Here are some ideas about what you could do together:

- Take them to (and stay to watch!) any sport or other activity they're involved in or enjoy watching.
- Take them to a concert and watch it together (don't just drop them off). Let them pick the artist once in a while, and try to resist commenting on the music if you don't like it.
- Listen. Set aside time on a semi-regular (but not strictly scheduled) basis and let them know you are available to listen to anything they have to say on any topic at all, whether it is something going on in their lives or the state of US politics. One conversation may lead to another that gets to the crux of what is worrying them at any specific time. Give advice only if they ask for it.
- Establish some regular shared activities or rituals. A ritual or tradition is pretty much anything that a family does together and proactively, as long as it is lifted above the monotonous routine of everyday life. Teenagers may complain about rituals but they'll also often be the first to object if they're cancelled. Order pizza on a Friday night, regularly attend a religious service, ride your bikes to your favourite cafe or have an annual holiday at the same special beach house.

- Have set times when technological devices, including the TV, are switched off and stay off. For example, it may be for an hour each side of meal times.
- Best of all, have a day when your teenager runs the day. This requires you to do exactly what they want you to do. Put away your devices, ignore the overflowing laundry basket, and focus solely on your teenager. Let them be the 'boss of the day'. Top off the day with a meal of their choice at their favourite cafe or restaurant.

Whatever you do, make sure that you physically engage with your teenager (e.g. offer to give them a massage, go for a swim/surf together, watch a movie on the couch together or play a video game together). Hugging can go by the wayside during adolescence. It's a pity, because many teens crave this closeness, and can develop 'skin hunger'.

Part 3

Common issues

In a 2008 study by Nancy Darling, an associate professor at Oberlin College, Ohio, a whopping 98 per cent of teenagers admitted lying to their parents (and perhaps the other 2 per cent just wouldn't admit it . . .). Out of thirty-six possible topics discussed with the teenagers, including drug use, dating and friends, the average teen admitted to lying about twelve of them. Another study, this time by the University of Amsterdam, showed that teenagers are the age group most likely to lie successfully, with an average of 2.8 lies told within the previous 24 hours.

While the strategies outlined in parts 1 and 2 of this book will help you to build a respectful and honest relationship with your teenager, we can't expect them to always be truthful – let's face it, no one is! Many things influence the decisions teenagers make and the situations they need to negotiate. Not everything is going to be in your control, and you may not know the full extent of what your teenager is up to.

Nevertheless, armed with the right information, parents can do a stellar job of 'drip feeding' information to their teens, when the moment is right, to help them make good decisions when the time comes.

The six chapters in this section highlight a broad range of factors that can impact your child's health and wellbeing, including school, bullying, mental health, alcohol and drug use, sex, and family breakdown And we tackle the one issue that is on every parent's hit list – the good, the bad and the ugly of technology.

Chapter 10
School

When your child tells you they're sick of school, they probably have better reasons than you thought. According to a 2014 report by the Organisation for Economic Co-operation and Development (OECD), Australian children spend considerably more time in school than in any of the thirty-four other OECD countries, including Korea, Japan, Finland, Sweden, Norway, the US and the UK. Over the duration of primary and lower secondary years, Australian children receive 10 120 hours of compulsory instruction compared to the OECD average of 7475 hours.

So you'd think with all those contact hours we'd be on the podium when it comes to academic performance. Well, think again. It's frankly baffling that young people in the countries regularly blitzing Australia academically do not spend nearly as much time in the classroom. For example, Finland only has students in the classroom for a measly 6327 hours in primary and lower secondary years and consistently comes at the top of international rankings for education systems. Similarly, Korean children spend only 6410 hours in the classroom. Something is not quite right!

The 2016 Progress in International Reading Literacy Study showed that our Year 4 students rank twenty-first in the world on reading achievement, below the Russian Federation, Poland, Latvia and Lithuania. The Trends in International Maths and Science Study shows that our Year 4 students were outperformed in mathematics by students in twenty-one other countries, including Ireland, England, the US, Singapore, Hong Kong and Korea. Only 9 per cent achieved the advanced international benchmark in mathematics, compared to 50 per cent in Singapore and 27 per cent in Northern Ireland. What's more, we have now been overtaken by a bunch of countries we were previously ahead of, including Slovenia, Hungary and Kazakhstan. We did slightly better in science – only seventeen countries crushed us academically.

So what's going on? Some commentators argue that the curriculum has been dumbed down and students are no longer taught to master the basics. Others blame a crowded curriculum whereby teachers have to teach everything from personal safety, cyber safety, road safety to wellness and, of course, how to be resilient. Still others argue nothing is being done to address the real reasons that our students underperform, which is that compared with overseas education systems, Australia has some of the highest rates of bullying, disruptive classrooms and badly behaved students. They also point to the impact that the mental health of teachers and principals has on their ability to stay in the job and teach effectively.

The Principal Health and Wellbeing Survey, conducted annually by the Australian Catholic University, found that in 2017, one in five principals was overwhelmed by workplace stress, almost half had faced threats of violence at work, and one in three had experienced actual violence. When it comes to classrooms, studies estimate that 30–50 per cent of teachers leave within the first five years in the job, citing excessive workloads (on average, full-time teachers self-report working 52–53 hours per week), 'high stakes' assessments (such as NAPLAN) and a lack of support and mentoring.

If you are a parent confronted and confused by this research, what – apart from moving to Finland – are you to do?

- When choosing a school for your son or daughter, find out as much as you can, and seek a fit between the school's strengths and your child's personality, temperament and interests. Be aware that you cannot predict the cohort that they will be learning with.
- Students will work for teachers they love. Parents play an important role in encouraging offspring to develop good relationships with their teachers. That said, remember that teachers like Mr Keating in *Dead Poets Society* are rare and tend to be found only in movies.
- If a teenager repeatedly complains about hating school, it is your job to find out why and to offer help. Make sure they know that you care about

their happiness, take their concerns seriously and want to work towards a resolution.

- If a young person is persistently unhappy at school, and it's not just that they don't like the colour of the uniform, consider alternative schools, home schooling, TAFE or, for older teens, letting them take a year off for travel or a job, even if it is between Year 11 and 12.
- Social media, mobile phones, giant televisions, and ever-evolving office hours contribute to the disappearance of family dinners. Study after study (yes, there are actually studies on this) demonstrate the usefulness of a regular evening meal around the table with no electronics – doing this can improve language skills, reduce the likelihood of substance misuse and improve academic results. Someone set the table!
- We need to keep the importance of the final years of school in perspective. It is not the be-all-and-end-all, but just one stage in a student's career. The success of their whole life does not revolve around what mark they get at the end of school. The research is again clear that students who succeed are focused, disciplined and work hard, but still manage to maintain a nice balance between work and play. Getting enough sleep, relaxation and exercise, eating sensibly and drinking plenty of H_2O all help maintain motivation. School should end with a bang, not a whimper! Celebrate at the end of the school year, not when the results come out.

Bear in mind that studying is made much easier if young people have a goal to work towards, are sure that they want to be at school and have chosen the right subjects (i.e. ones they enjoy and are even passionate about). Encourage your teen to meet with a careers counsellor. As the Roman philosopher Seneca once said, 'When a man does not know what port he is headed for, no wind is the right wind.'

EDUCATION FOR ALL?

School is less likely to be a major problem academically for girls than for boys. Statistics tell us that girls generally work harder than boys, behave better in class and perform better in most school subjects. But it doesn't mean that school is necessarily a better place for girls. A study from the Wales Institute of Social & Economic Research, Data & Methods of 1500 pupils showed that while girls outperform boys academically, they are less happy at school. Three times the number of girls felt that they didn't 'belong' at school, and a quarter felt worried at school, compared to 16 per cent of boys. So while they may be performing better, the school years can be fraught with feelings of doubt, anxiety and lack of belonging.

Programme for International Student Assessment results show that girls do better in reading in all countries, whereas boys do better in mathematics in most (but not all) countries. Researchers agree that aptitude is not gendered, so what causes these gaps? Australian researchers Julie Moschion and Deborah Cobb-Clark examined the gap using longitudinal data and concluded that parental expectations and investment in education were important factors, as well as an individual child's school readiness. They also found, interestingly, that the gender gap in reading was evident *prior* to the school years, so reading to and encouraging reading with boys in the early years really is important.

In terms of aptitude for certain subjects, a large-scale University of Melbourne study of 58 000 students shows that in Victoria, boys are five times more likely than girls to study physics, nine times more likely to study information technology, and twice as likely to study advanced maths in years 11 and 12. This is even when girls outperform boys in these subjects – so girls need to be encouraged to study these subjects, too.

SINGLE SEX VS CO-ED

The old chestnut of single sex versus co-education still causes fearsome debates on talkback radio. When you look carefully at the research, however, it's surprising to find that the jury is actually out on whether single-sex schools or co-ed schools are preferable in terms of academic performance. It depends on the type of academic measures you are interested in, and what other things you are looking for, such as location, facilities, discipline and bullying policies and academic reputation, as well as knowing your own child and what will best suit them. For example, if girls are at a single-sex school, they tend to be more confident about their ability as learners in subjects such as mathematics and physics, and feel less constrained about participating in classroom discussions.

Projections from the ABS show that the popularity of single-sex schools is declining to the extent that if the trend continues, single-sex independent schools won't exist by 2035. There has been a growing trend in recent years for single-sex schools to convert to co-ed, with justifications that having both boys and girls in the classroom helps teach mutual respect. Some schools have compromised by having separate classes for girls and boys for maths and English; this is called parallel education and recognises the diverse educational needs of boys and girls.

Consistently, research finds that teachers are the most influential factor in academic achievement, rather than factors such as single sex versus co-educational schools. Giving teachers support, access to professional development and continuous learning, and encouragement to take risks lead to greater satisfaction for them, which can only benefit students. It is also worth noting that several studies have now shown that a teacher's gender has no measurable effect on students' academic achievement.

BUT THE BOYS . . .

There is, though, something fundamentally amiss when it comes to boys' education. Their lag behind girls in academic achievement began more than fifty years ago and still remains. Generally speaking, boys read less than girls, have a shorter attention span when it comes to school and homework, and are massively overrepresented in school detentions, suspensions and expulsions. They are more likely to leave school early, across all types of schools. We are also seeing far more boys in remedial classes and in behaviour management units in our schools throughout the country. A growing proportion of young men are not working to their potential and are not motivated to perform academically in the way that their female peers are.

In the 2005 edition of this book I predicted that if this situation continued, within a decade, seven out of ten students enrolled at university would be women. In some cases this has become true; for example, 72 per cent of students at the Australian Catholic University, and 71 per cent at the University of Notre Dame are women. While this can be attributed to a certain extent to the large number of health and education courses at these institutions, the total average across all universities is still in favour of women (56 per cent). Female students have outnumbered their male counterparts in Australian universities since 1987. In 2014 the sex ratio for higher education students was just 80 males per 100 females, compared to 269 males per 100 females in 1970. This imbalance widened between 2004 and 2012 (from 84.1 to 79.3 males per 100 females). What's worse, 2017 figures reveal that one in three Australian university students are dropping out prior to the completion of their course, and they are more likely to be male.

Australian educators continue to engage in passionate debate about how to better address boys' needs at school and get them back to learning. The truth is that many boys don't feel safe, valued or listened to at school. This problem starts in primary school, where we see more and more boys who regard academic achievement as a feminine trait. Many boys believe that doing well at school is what girls do. The longer these boys stay at school, the more likely they are to be disaffected from the learning process.

What has changed over the last thirty years that might account for this situation? My theory is twofold. First, there have been changes in schools and in popular culture that have contributed to the general impression about schools and education. For example, popular songs often reflect the zeitgeist or spirit of the time. In 1960, singer Sam Cooke released a song called 'Wonderful World', which became a number one smash hit. In the song, Sam says he believes that improving himself – getting an A instead of a B – will raise his status in the eyes of the girl he seeks to impress. By contrast, these days, songs that have schools as a subject are more likely to be damning. Take for example the 2015 YouTube hit by Boyinaband titled 'Don't Stay in School', which has amassed more than 23 million views. It outlines the singer's frustration with what he learned in school (e.g. dissecting a frog, defining isotopes) as opposed to 'real world' knowledge (e.g. how to get a job, how to vote). (I'll leave it to you to wade through the comments and videos in response – if nothing else the video certainly opened up an interesting, and divided, conversation.)

The second issue is that education has undergone profound change. There has been an acceleration of the early academic curriculum – if you walked into a classroom thirty years ago, 4-year-olds would have been singing, dancing, drawing . . . participating in a diverse range of activities and a little bit of formal didactic instruction, which would have been a small part of the day. Today preschool looks a lot like Grade 1: children are sitting at desks learning to read and write. These changes have occurred without reference to the significant differences in the way in which boys and girls learn; for example, that boys often like to learn through movement and visuals.

It is not developmentally appropriate, nor is it likely to be hugely successful, to ask 5-year-old boys to sit still and be quiet. Girls are more likely to succeed with this, and in turn will be more likely to receive praise. The message that boys get from an early age is that doing well at school means being more like a girl. The problem is that girls don't want to be like boys and vice versa.

HOW TO HELP BOYS (AND GIRLS) GET MORE OUT OF SCHOOL

While we are waiting for schools to take up the challenge of creating boy-friendly learning environments (like appointing a boys' education coordinator to give the issue a profile and push some of the research recommendations), there are a few things worth knowing. The following recommendations come from chatting to a variety of educators who have spent years investigating these issues, which might help you at home. It might even be worthwhile asking the school principal politely whether the school has considered them. Change will only come if parents (who are ultimately the consumers) know about what is being said in educational circles and actively advocate.

1. **Delay school starting ages.** One of the features of Finnish education is a 'late' start. Believe it or not, the children don't step inside what we would call primary school until they hit seven. Prior to this the kindies/daycare centres in Finland do not ram maths, reading or writing down their throats (in fact they get nothing on this formally until they begin primary school). Instead, the emphasis is on creative play, wellbeing and building social and emotional competencies. The priority is to create social beings who have the rudiments of conflict resolution, anger management, problem solving and decision making. The result is that by the time Finnish children start school they know how to obtain, maintain and retain friendships and there is a focus on the 'joy of learning', language enhancement and communication. The best thing of all, from a wellbeing stance, is that at least ninety minutes of outdoor play a day is encouraged.

2. **Change school start times.** The time at which the sleep hormone melatonin is released varies with age: during adolescence, secretion begins late at night and continues until about 8 a.m. As a result the sleep rhythm of a teenager can lag by two to three hours compared to an adult, placing it out of step with social expectations, such as early school start times. Adults often think that if teenagers would only go to bed earlier, they'd be able to wake up clear-headed and ready for school, but the research indicates otherwise. The internal clock of adolescents means they don't

find themselves ready to sleep until late at night, a pattern similar to that of rodents (and I'll leave that comparison right there).

I believe school start times should be moved to as late as 11 a.m. to combat a sleep-deprivation crisis among young people in Australia, who are losing on average ten hours' sleep a week due to their sleep patterns. Neuroscientists like Russell Foster of Oxford University and Steven Lockley of Harvard Medical School are among a growing number of scientists pushing for change in understanding students' sleep patterns. They argue that children aged 8 to 10 should start school at 8.30 a.m. or later, 16-year-olds should start at 10 a.m. and 18-year-olds at 11 a.m. The recommendations arise from a more comprehensive understanding of teenager's internal body clocks, which determine optimum levels of concentration, wakefulness and work ability. Ignoring the natural circadian rhythms of students leads to their increased irritability, exhaustion, frustration, anxiety, weight gain and hypertension and thereby means they are more prone to substance misuse and risk-taking.

3. **Schools should provide healthy food.** Back in my day, too many school cafeterias looked and operated almost like fast-food restaurants where students got cheap, fast and unhealthy meals. Teaching students about 'brain foods' (e.g. wholegrains, eggs, blueberries) is a good strategy, especially in the senior years. Some boarding schools, like the Dilworth School in

New Zealand, have banned sugar from meals given to students. Some schools, for example in Iceland and Sweden, have turned almost completely to organic foods, and others are growing their own fruits and vegetables, where students water them and learn about nature. A great example of this in Australia is the Stephanie Alexander kitchen gardens, currently delivered in 800 schools around the country. Students grow, harvest, prepare and share the food.

4. **Physical education (PE) should be mandatory for all age groups.** With obesity rates reaching stratospheric levels, governments must heed the calls of public health experts to make school environments healthier. One way to achieve this is to make physical activity mandatory – in many secondary schools now, PE classes stop at Year 9 or 10. Keeping active is undeniably positive for students, and schools should recognise the link between regular activity and successful learning.

5. **Ensure teachers are better qualified.** All teachers in Finland are selected from the top 10 per cent of applicants and they must have a Masters degree, which is fully subsidised. They are regarded as having a similar status to doctors and lawyers.

6. **Get rid of the National Assessment Program – Literacy and Numeracy (NAPLAN).** This program was established in 2008, and there has been no evidence of overall improvement throughout the years it

has been running. In fact, Year 7 and 9 literacy marks have decreased since the start of this worthless test.

A Melbourne University survey of teachers found that 90 per cent of teachers reported that students felt stressed before taking the test. Others argue that four of the five domains in NAPLAN are focused on literacy and that's a traditional area of strength for girls, who typically enjoy a word-rich learning style, meaning boys are less likely to do well.

Importantly, the results aren't current. Delivered up to half a year after the test, NAPLAN results are practically useless as a feedback tool for students. It is worth noting that children in Finland are not measured at all for the first six years of their education, while NAPLAN is conducted at Years 3, 5, 7 and 9. There is only one mandatory standardised test in Finland, taken when children are 16, and 93 per cent of students graduate from high school.

7. **Last but not least, we need to create environments where students feel secure, valued and connected.** Until this happens, we will continue to see unacceptable levels of depression, anxiety and self-harm.

If you believe your child is isolated, bullied or at risk in any other way, talk to their teacher or the year-level coordinator. Parents and teachers tend to interact far less in secondary school than in the primary years, so it's important that you take the initiative and make it happen. There is clearly much that can and should be done. Get up and be an advocate for your child.

Chapter 11
Technology

Unless you have been living in a cave (and probably even then), you would know that most young people these days live much of their lives online. In fact, a Roy Morgan survey of children aged 6–13 years shows that in mid-2016 the internet finally surpassed television in terms of how our offspring elected to spend their time. This must come as a shock to a generation of parents raised on a steady diet of *Gilligan's Island*, *The Love Boat* and *Young Talent Time*. The Australian Communications and Media Authority reports that more than four in five teenagers aged 12–17 years are regularly online.

Today's 'screenagers' are unarguably the most tech-savvy generation ever. They are probably better than you with the devices in your home. But there is a paradox here. This tech savviness is often accompanied by a brain that is more accelerator than brake, as discussed in Chapter 2. Impulsivity, a desire to be accepted and a susceptibility to peer influence are all characteristics of adolescence that can lead to problems in the online world. Bill Belsey, the creator of www.cyberbullying.ca, the world's first website about cyber bullying, argues that technology represents a perfect storm, where the immature teenage brain meets a technology that is in the moment and of the moment.

How well I recall the days of the old fixed landline, with its massive handset and its lack of privacy, that allowed your parents to pick up the other handset and demand you get off the phone. It's little wonder so many parents are scrambling to keep up. So what do contemporary parents need to know?

ADOLESCENTS USE TECHNOLOGY DIFFERENTLY FROM US

Understand that your offspring will use technology in ways that are unique to this generation. Schools fundamentally regard technology as useful for accessing new knowledge and learning. Young people have also discovered that technology is a brilliant tool to help them fast-track many of the key developmental tasks of adolescence. In particular it helps fulfill the desire to be with peers, emancipation from adult carers, and identity formation. In short, technology is a vital part of young people's social lives and how they build their identity. Where we might differentiate between being online and 'real life', it's all one world to them.

ONLINE DANGERS

While the internet provides many valuable and engaging opportunities, it can also enable exposure to offensive and illegal online material. The Office of eSafety lists several areas of grave concern when it comes to keeping our children safe online, such as cyber bullying, hate sites, sexting, mobile phone safety and easy access to pornography.

The good news is that all parents can decrease the likelihood of exposure by implementing a variety of online safeguards and parental controls. The technology and the danger involved will change so reviewing these plans frequently is crucial.

Most parents may not know what the acronyms 'DM me' or 'GNIFOC' mean. 'DM me' means 'direct message me' and is a common way young people can have private conversations. 'GNIFOC' means 'get naked in front of camera'. It is hard as a parent to keep current when it comes to internet slang, the latest apps and their inherent dangers. Even to an interested observer, language and favourite apps can change in the blink of an eye.

It is not just the language but the apps themselves that can pose dangers. Parents can keep up to date by googling 'iparent', or bookmarking the Office of the eSafety Commissioner website. This will help you stay abreast of the latest developments and dangers – so you can make an informed choice about whether your offspring should be using a particular app or website. Never ever be conned/manipulated/hoodwinked by the cry, 'But everyone else has it', because while some may, the majority don't, and the ones who do might not have responsible parents.

SOCIAL MEDIA

As far as the social media companies (most based in the US) are concerned, the question of when to allow young people to open their own social media account is very straightforward. They are obliged to abide by the US federal law, specifically the Children's Online Privacy Protection Act (1998), known as COPPA, which restricts the online collection of personal information related to persons under 13. Strictly speaking, the minimum age for opening a Facebook, Instagram, Twitter, Pinterest, Tumblr or Snapchat account is 13, while Kik users under 17 need permission from adult carers. Some sites, such as Tinder, request that you be at least 18 to open an account. However, while social media sites state that they will deregister an account if they are told the user is under 13, this rarely occurs.

Psychologists quite rightly point out that age does not define maturity and the technical age limit imposed by COPPA and the social media companies is completely arbitrary. As such, it is a parent's responsibility to think about the psychological maturity, personality and temperament of their offspring and then evaluate whether they believe their child has the social and emotional skills for social media, such as judging what to share and with whom.

My own clinical experience has demonstrated that some 13-year-olds have the psychological maturity of a gnat. In my view, all parents should exercise caution when deciding whether their child should have a social media account and, if in doubt, seek expert guidance. Even so, discussions with primary school principals across Australia reveal with absolute clarity that expert advice and rules imposed by social media companies are being largely ignored by parents and by young people frantic to join peers online. Many parents try to stick to a philosophy of 'Not until high school' and resist the pester power for as long as possible, but as more and more parents cave in, this proves more difficult.

Once an account has been opened, remain engaged by monitoring and supervising your offspring. Make it a condition of them having the account that they 'friend' you – or whatever the specific app's lingo is – and that they have to share their password. This way you can stay involved with their online behaviour. The bottom line is that if your child joins Snapchat, Facebook, Instagram, Twitter, Pinterest, YouTube or Tumblr, so should you.

While some parents rejoice in the hours of distraction that social media provides their children, others feel that it robs them of quality time with their sons and daughters. Stories abound of family holidays being ruined as teenagers spend what should be family time huddled over a device.

Other parents are concerned about the impact of social media on young people's sense of reality. Many accounts are full of highly edited and curated images from the likes of Kardashians and Jenners, and it behoves all adult carers to remind their children that an Instagram life is not real.

MUSICAL.LY – A CASE STUDY FOR THE CONTEMPORARY PARENT

At first glance musical.ly seems like a fun, karaoke-type app. The description on the iTunes store says musical.ly is the world's 'largest creative platform'. The platform allows you to make your own videos and impress your friends; essentially, it becomes a popularity contest where the number of 'likes' tells you how popular you are. It appears relatively benign, and has over 60 million users, who are encouraged to mime and dance to music they choose from within the app or create their own music videos.

So how could this app be detrimental? Closer examination of the warnings on the side bar of the iTunes store state the app has:

- Infrequent/Mild Profanity or Crude Humour
- Infrequent/Mild Sexual Content and Nudity
- Infrequent/Mild Mature/Suggestive Themes
- Infrequent/Mild Cartoon or Fantasy Violence
- Infrequent/Mild Alcohol, Tobacco, or Drug Use or References.

In addition to this, there is potential for bullying and harassment in comments.

Musical.ly and other apps also have default privacy settings that automatically allow location sharing and open communication with users. An Illinois father drew attention to this in 2017 when he warned parents that a stranger had asked his 7-year-old daughter to send shirtless photos of herself via the app's messaging feature. If your children are using this app (and others – this should be a general rule), make sure that you change settings to private, hide location information, and talk to your child about ways to avoid giving clues to their whereabouts (e.g. never filming in school uniform).

It is almost inevitable that kids see and view many things online outside of a parent's control these days. But there are ways to make the online environment safer for your child if you take the time and effort. You wouldn't allow your child to hang out in a dangerous place offline, so why would you allow them to do so online?

PARENTAL CONTROLS

Tools such as Net Nanny, Qustodio and Kaspersky Safe Kids help parents oversee and set boundaries on what their children do online. The early introduction of these programs by adult carers is infinitely preferable to a later introduction after the digital horse has bolted.

While none of these programs is 100 per cent successful at stopping access to unsuitable content, their value lies in acting as a catalyst for a conversation with young people concerning what they do online. The most successful programs seem to have been developed for computer platforms, and while some exist for smartphones, tablets and gaming consoles, further parental guidance is necessary with these.

These programs can stop young people from accessing specific websites and apps, filter content (e.g. sexual content), and allow parents to monitor use, including what sites are accessed, for how long and how frequently. Most importantly, they can be used to set time limits, blocking access after a set period – this is useful if parents are going out and want to limit the time spent on a game or on social media. Parents can also alter the settings to reflect each child's age.

The software should never be a substitute for regular discussion about staying safe online; for example, talking about not accepting files or opening email attachments from people they don't know, treating others with respect, and never ever posting anything online that they would not want the 4 Ps to see: parents, principal, police or paedophile. It is important to note that the software is more effective at identifying sites with 'adult' content than those websites that incite self-harm, eating disorders, violence, drugs, gambling, racism and terrorism. These types of software can also struggle to detect material within social media sites and messaging services, including video messaging services like Skype.

SEARCH ENGINES

Google, Bing and Yahoo are the search engines most frequently used by young people to research assignments or to explore online, but with that open access comes the risk of exposure to adult material.

The office of eSafety offers six tips to searching safely, summarised here:

1. Use child-friendly search engines (e.g. Google's Safe Search Kids, KidzSearch, KidsClick, KidRex and Swiggle), which filter out inappropriate sites and material.
2. Use safe search settings. The most commonly used search engines have safe search settings to block

inappropriate, explicit and adult-oriented content from search results.

3. Protect devices. Using the internet exposes all devices to malware, systems designed to steal the data or disrupt the functioning of your device. Having regularly updated security software guards against this.

4. Bookmark preferred websites. Your kids can go directly to favourite websites without having to first conduct a search to locate them online.

5. Check the website's safety rating before visiting it by using online search tools that help identify malicious websites.

6. Talk about safe searching with your child, including the kind of websites they can view.

WHAT TO DO IF THEY SEE INAPPROPRIATE MATERIAL

If your child has been exposed to objectionable material, whether unintentionally or on purpose, have a discussion about what they have seen. Reassure them that it is okay for them to talk to you about anything they find disturbing. You can also report any online material that you think is offensive or illegal to the eSafety Commissioner (www.esafety.gov.au/complaints-and-reporting/offensive-and-illegal-content-complaints).

Chapter 12
Bullying

Extensive research has consistently demonstrated the pervasiveness of bullying in schools and its far-reaching detrimental effects on students, both in Australia and internationally.

School bullying involves the repeated psychological, emotional, social or physical harassment of one student by another (though teachers and parents can also be bullies or targets too). It may be verbal (e.g. face to face, or via phone, text or email messages), non-verbal (e.g. body language), or physical and/or antisocial (e.g. gossip or exclusion). It can vary from direct to indirect harassment, from minor irritation to major assault, from 'just having a bit of fun' to breaking the law. Face-to-face bullying, which is verbal teasing that may escalate to physical violence, is still alive and well in the digital age, and it is still the most prominent form of bullying.

School bullying is widely viewed as an urgent social, health and education concern. All parents should expect schools to have the following:

- A bullying policy on the school website
- A comprehensive definition of bullying, including listing what it is not considered bullying
- An overall ethos or declaration around rights and responsibilities, such as the Kandersteg Declaration, in a prominent position, such as the foyer of the school
- A reference in their policy to the role of the bystander (bullying occurs within a group context, with peers present as onlookers in the vast majority of bullying interactions, so bystanders can have active, diverse and involved roles in the bullying process, from facilitating to inhibiting bullying)
- A reference in their policy to the National Safe Schools Framework – the NSSF is the pre-eminent policy document guiding schools in Australia in respect to school bullying
- Regular reviews of their policy using the Safe Schools Toolkit (which has an online audit tool)
- Surveys of students and parents about bullying using valid and reliable tools
- Regular, up-to-date professional development and training for staff – research shows that the implementation of a whole-school bullying policy is greatly enhanced by such training
- A representative group responsible for overseeing the school's safety and wellbeing initiatives, made up of staff, students, parents and carers

All schools should have an electronic 'bully box' installed as part of the fight to combat schoolyard bullying. This is simply a school-administered email address that is checked daily and is promoted to students, advising them that if they experience bullying and/or witness an event, they can confidentially report the incident to the school authorities.

All students have a legal right to feel safe at school. Bullying should not be dismissed as a harmless schoolyard rite of passage. It is a major problem in Australian schools and has serious consequences over the short, medium and long terms. And despite what you may have heard, it happens in all schools – state, Catholic and independent. Findings from the Australian Covert Bullying Prevalence Study at the Child Health Promotion Research Centre, Edith Cowan University, show that one in four young people are bullied, while 83 per cent of youth perpetrators attack their victims in person and via the internet. One in four students in grades 4–9 are bullied frequently. Year 5 and Year 8 students face higher risks of being bullied than their younger and older peers. Older students are more likely to engage in cyber bullying than younger students. Many bullies don't consciously realise their behaviours are abusive, but unconsciously they know they are taking away their target's power. Other Australian research suggests that one in six students are bullied weekly and bothered by it: 54 per cent of Year 7 students say they feel unsafe at school. Sadly, many believe that bullying cannot be stopped, and almost half the victims tell no-one that it's happened. Of those who do, most tell their friends first, then Mum and Dad, and teachers last of all. We know that boys and girls are equally involved and that bullying by girls is more likely to be subtle and psychological, involving teasing, taunting and isolation.

The reason bullying continues to occur is largely because those who observe it choose to do nothing (eight out of ten bystanders do not intervene). There is an unwritten school commandment that 'Thou shalt not dob!', not least because most students believe that nothing can be done or that speaking up will only make matters worse. This, of course, plays directly into the hands of the bully.

HOW TO TELL IF YOUR CHILD IS BEING BULLIED

Parents have a key role to play in relation to bullying – both in recognising if their child is being bullied and in reporting it. Be vigilant for the signs, which include your child:

- being frightened of walking to or from school, or changing their usual routine
- being unwilling to go to school at all and/or beginning to skip school
- showing a decline in schoolwork
- coming home regularly with belongings destroyed or damaged
- regularly 'losing' possessions, food or money
- becoming withdrawn, distressed or anxious
- crying themselves to sleep or having nightmares

- becoming unreasonable or aggressive
- giving improbable excuses to explain any of the above.

Here are some dos and don'ts if your child is being bullied:

- **Do** act right away. Your teenager needs you to advocate on their behalf.
- **Do** remember that schools have a duty of care towards their students. Contact the school (by phone, email, or seek a face-to-face meeting) as soon as possible. If you are unsatisfied with the results, go directly to the principal. It is also a good idea to keep a written record of all phone conversations and meetings you attend.
- **Don't** attempt to contact the bully's parents – it's not your job. Leave it to the school, and take it up with the principal if they don't follow through.
- **Don't** tell your child to fight back, because that can lead to much more serious harm and even accusations that *they* are the bully.

Since writing the 2005 edition of this book, my views on bullying have consolidated. It is clear that victims are at high risk of depression, anxiety and suicide, while perpetrators could end up with antisocial personality disorders leading to violent outbursts. It is more important than ever before for parents to make sure they know what is going on in their child's life at school. Research shows that children who are chronically victimised at school but have supportive home environments with open lines of communication are less likely to consider suicide. This means that parents can play a critical role in supporting children who are being bullied, especially as many parents say their schools are non-responsive.

My advice now is that if parents go through the normal school hierarchy and get nowhere, they should hire a lawyer and get back in there and hold the school accountable. The school has a legal duty of care to provide a safe environment for children to learn in. Failing to provide that environment is a breach of their duty of care.

WHAT IF YOUR CHILD IS DOING THE BULLYING?

Parents who discover their child has been engaging in bullying behaviour need to be proactive in nipping this in the bud.

If your offspring is identified as a bully, it is important to seek help in changing their behaviour. Being a bully has been found to interfere with academic performance, learning, friendships, work, intimate relationships, income and mental health. Young people who bully others are more likely to damage property or steal, misuse substances and get in trouble with the law. It may also be an outward sign of depression, so seeking a professional assessment is a good idea. The Australian Institute of Family Studies suggests four important things you can do if the school tells you that your child has been bullying others. These are adapted below.

Step 1. Manage your reactions and get the facts

Don't blow a gasket! It is normal to feel defensive or a desire to head down to school and throttle your child. Instead, try to stay calm and look at the situation rationally. Thank the school for informing you and respond by assuring them that once you have confirmed the veracity of the allegations, you will do everything you can to support the school, encourage your offspring to recognise the error of their ways and help them make different choices.

Step 2. Take time to process the information

If the incident is serious, schools are obliged to involve the police, so try and jot down as much information as you can. Note the name, title and contact details of the person who notifies you of the bullying. Ensure that you make a time to follow up in order to be kept abreast of any developments in the school's investigation and any actions that you may be required to take. For many parents this news is like a loss experience, so give yourself time to 'grieve' and process your thoughts and feelings. Telling a close friend or partner and reflecting with them will help with this.

Step 3. Talk with your child

This may be a challenging and demanding conversation, so here are some tips:

- Try to stay composed. Inform your child that the school has made contact, and that you have not jumped to any conclusions but that you need to know the truth. If you remain open-minded, calm and amicable, you can create an environment where the young person feels able to admit the things that they now regret and share their thinking at the time. Avoid using strong-arm tactics (e.g. name and shame, physical punishment), as this reaction often models bullying itself.
- Reassure them that everyone makes mistakes, and that irrespective of what happened, you will support them. It is important to directly ask your child:
  - Do you know what they are talking about?
  - What happened?
  - Is any of this true?
- If they tell you what the other child did, tell them that you want to hear that, but you also want to hear what *they* did. Ask your child:
  - Can you help me understand why the other kid sees it their way?
  - How would you feel if they did that to you?
- Find out more about the bullying. In particular, it's important to understand that students who engage in bullying behaviour are often also victims. This doesn't mean that the bullying behaviour should be minimised or ignored, but it is an important part of the fact gathering. Ask your child:

- Have you been bullied?
- How long has this been going on for?
- Are there several students involved or just one?

Explore what may be triggering the bullying behaviour in your child, whether it is in response to anything, when it occurs and where.

Parents have an obligation to let their child know that bullying is not acceptable, is against the values, attitudes and beliefs of the family and that it must stop. Let them know that this is a serious matter and that you are going to work with the school to ensure that it doesn't continue. Don't finger wag – a relatively short, simple statement will get your point across better; for example, 'I need you to know that bullying is unacceptable, and it must stop.'

Step 4. Work to resolve the situation

Don't give in to the temptation to downplay or excuse the behaviour as a one-off. The aim is to try and objectively assess the risk and protective factors in your child's various worlds, such as their peers, family and school. Brainstorm the conceivable reasons for your child's actions. Discuss these with your child or a psychologist to come up with alternative strategies to minimise risk factors and increase protective factors.

Read the school's bullying policies and ensure that your child understands how and why they are in breach of the policy. Once the school has handed down a sanction, take the opportunity to have a discussion with your child's teachers, year-level coordinator or school welfare coordinator. Seek advice from them on what role you can play in supporting the school. Indicate your willingness to be informed and be involved in any supervision and monitoring that they deem necessary.

Chapter 13
Mental health

As a child and adolescent psychologist, I am more worried about our young people and their future than ever before. Allow me to explain why.

The latest ABS statistics on causes of death, which at the time of writing were for 2016, tell us that the suicide rate for 15–24-year-old young men is at its highest level in ten years. It is at catastrophic levels for Aboriginal and Torres Strait Islander young people, triple the rate of non-Indigenous young people. Every eighteen hours in 2016, one young Australian male aged 15–24 died by suicide – a total of 491 young men that year. The number of young women aged 15–29 who ended their lives in 2016 was more than double the number in 2006. Suicide was the leading cause of death in children aged 5–17.

Research tells us that 75 per cent of psychological problems in adults start before the age of 25, so this is a hugely concerning trend considering that we know mental illness is highly prevalent in those who commit suicide. One in four (roughly 750 000) young Australians currently have a mental illness, including young people with a substance use disorder. Suicide remains the biggest killer of young Australians, accounting for the deaths of more young people than car accidents. In this supposedly lucky country, the mental health of our young people is worse than it was for their parents at the same age.

This is a dire situation. But what really worry me are two reports released in late 2017, which you may not have seen but send shivers up my spine because they outline the prospect of an even bleaker future.

The first was a report by Mission Australia, which surveyed more than 24 000 young people and asked them to rank how concerned they had been about a number of issues in the past year. Nationally, the top three issues of concern were coping with stress, school or study problems, and body image, with 45.3 per cent of the respondents indicating that they were either extremely concerned or very concerned about coping with stress, 35.6 per cent extremely concerned or very concerned about school or study problems, and 31.1 per cent extremely concerned or very concerned about body image. The proportion of girls concerned about each of these issues was much higher than the proportion of boys.

Each year since the survey began, the proportion of young people who indicate that they don't know how to deal with stress has increased. Surely this means parents and schools need to do more to prepare young people for life. There is a clear need for social and emotional competencies such as anger management, conflict resolution and problem solving to become part of the curriculum before it is too late.

The second report came from the Australian Psychological Society – the APS Compass for Life wellbeing survey. It too painted a pretty grim picture of young people and their resilience and capacity to face, overcome, be transformed and strengthened by adversity.

The APS report found that young Australians had significantly low scores on engagement, positive emotion and overall wellbeing. They scored much higher on loneliness than people aged 35 and over – amazing considering how connected we assume they are in the age of social media. One in six respondents said they were dissatisfied with their lives and future outlook, and only 45 per cent had a strong sense of belonging to their community. This sense of belonging is key in resilience research, so this finding should be extremely worrying to all working with young people in health, education and welfare.

The data also suggests that young Australians are dropping the ball when it comes to the fundamental building blocks of wellbeing – namely sleep, exercise and diet. A paper in the well-respected *Journal of Physical Activity and Health* reported in 2016 that Australian children are among the least active in the world, ranking 21 out of 38 countries, with fewer than one in five children aged 5–17 meeting the recommended sixty minutes of physical activity each day. Fewer than one in four Grade 6 students have mastered physical milestones such as catching, throwing, sprinting, jumping and side galloping.

As far as sleep is concerned, our young people seem to be in the grip of a mass sleep-deprivation pandemic, with only one in three teenagers reporting regularly getting a good night's sleep according to the APS wellbeing survey. One in ten teenagers reported that they get a good night's sleep once a week or less often.

Figures from the Australian Health Survey, run by the ABS, show that less than 1 per cent of 12–18-year-olds usually met their recommended number of serves of vegetables and legumes or beans (five serves a day). Less than 2 per cent consumed the recommended 3.5 serves a day of dairy food. Things are slightly better when it comes to fruit – around one third met the recommendation of two serves per day. Australian teenagers do excel at one nutrition measure, however – three in four exceed the guidelines for daily sugar intake. This is mainly thanks to sugar-sweetened drinks.

We cannot afford to keep going this way. While awareness about mental illness has increased, it is critical that we don't mistake this for meaningful political action on the issue. We need to do far more than just talk, tweet and post about how catastrophic the situation is.

In primary care, there is an annual cap of ten sessions of psychological care under Medicare Benefits Schedule rules (reduced in 2011 from the original eighteen sessions). Why are we, as a nation, rationing mental health services to young people who are our future? If you did that for heart disease, cancer or diabetes there would be an outcry. Mental illness is a key public health issue in

Australia that is at a crisis point and demands the same attention as physical health issues.

The groups that I am most worried about are:

1. **Final year school students.** Stress levels of Year 12 students are out of control. As mentioned, the 2017 Mission Australia youth survey named school and study problems the second most concerning issue for the 24055 young people who took the survey, for the fifth year in a row. A 2017 survey of final-year students from a range of schools in Sydney showed high levels of psychological morbidity. Of the 722 students surveyed, 42 per cent registered anxiety symptoms at a level of severity to warrant clinical intervention. This proportion is nearly twice the population norm and significantly more than in earlier studies.

   Of the total survey group, 16 per cent of students reported extremely severe levels of anxiety, and 37 per cent registered above-average levels of stress. While stress, anxiety and pressure levels were high among girls, they were even more elevated in girls who had been labelled as gifted. Interestingly, these findings were not confined to one ethnic group but were constant across a range of cultural groups.

   Many regard the pressure students face in South Korea and other Asian countries as excessive, but students in this study reported academic pressure rates that were similar to those reported by some studies in Asian schools. Over half felt that the expectations put on them in Year 12 were excessive. The main sources of this stress were workload (50 per cent), expectations to perform (26 per cent) and importance of exams (22 per cent). Stress and anxiety were highest in students labelled gifted and talented.

2. **LGBTIQ young people.** The second group that seem to be at high risk are gender variant and sexuality diverse young people, who, the research suggests, are subject to different forms of discrimination with adverse impacts (socio-cultural, educational, political, and legal) on their health and wellbeing.

Particularly worrying are the rates of self-harm and suicidal ideation in this group. A national survey of more than 1000 16–27-year-olds who identified as gender variant or sexually diverse, conducted by the University of Western Sydney, showed that 41 per cent had thought about self-harm and/or suicide, 33 per cent had already engaged in self-harm and 16 per cent had attempted to end their lives. Disturbingly, many reported repeated harassment, violence, marginalisation, ostracism from peers and rejection from families, often resulting in feelings of hopelessness, isolation and of internalised homophobia or transphobia. Almost two-thirds of the LGBTIQ young people surveyed experienced some form of homophobia and/or transphobia, with some reporting multiple forms of abuse: 64 per cent verbal, 18 per cent physical, and 32 per cent experienced other types of homophobia and transphobia.

3. **Young women.** The last group that warrants special attention are young women. Navigating the journey from childhood to adulthood has always been tough for teenage girls, many of whom have to deal with a combination of skin breakouts, menstruation, cascading hormones, peer pressure, emotional intensity, excruciating insecurities, and a mosh pit of sexuality and vulnerability. But a whole new raft of risk factors, along with the rise of social media, seem to have created a generation of 13- and 14-year-old girls in crisis.

Put aside the fact that one in five teenage girls are on anxiety medication, and one in twelve will develop an eating disorder; as already mentioned, suicide rates are higher than ever before. Furthermore, there has been a dramatic increase in the hospitalisation of young Australian women who have intentionally harmed themselves. Figures released by the Australian Institute of Health and Welfare show that in 2010–11, there were more than 26 000 hospitalisations for self-harm across Australia. The majority of those treated were women, and the most marked difference between boys and girls was in the 15–19-year-old age group, where the rate for girls was almost triple that of boys. Over a 10-year period, intentional poisonings and overdoses among young women rose significantly and the number of cases of self-harm using a sharp object more than doubled.

HOW DO I KNOW IF THERE IS A PROBLEM WITH MY TEENAGER?

The general consensus is that mood swings and irritability are a normal part of being a teenager. To some extent this is true, but generalised ideas about teens are not helpful for parents and carers trying to identify and respond to potentially more serious problems.

Let's look at some examples of the three groups I am most concerned about.

> Amelia was renowned for her diligence with her
> schoolwork, which was always completed on time
> and to perfection. Her parents were so proud of
> her commitment that Amelia often heard them in
> conversation with friends and other family members
> about how well she was doing. In Year 12, however,
> Amelia's parents began noticing that she was constantly
> on edge and increasingly less engaged with the things
> she used to love doing, like going for a walk around
> the park and going to the movies with friends. If she
> was asked to attend family events, she was never really
> 'there' with the family, and seemed to often be on the
> brink of tears.

Three things to communicate to Amelia are:

1. Amelia is not the sum total of her mark at the end of Year 12 – there are lots of ways to be successful other than getting a high mark at school.
2. Amelia needs to know that her parents will love

her and be there for her no matter what happens in Year 12 – teenagers need to feel unconditional love.

3. Amelia's studies need to be balanced with enough sleep, exercise and healthy foods – spending time on this will actually make her more efficient, not less.

There are a number of apps that Amelia may find useful to help combat the feelings of stress and anxiety. These include:

- ReachOut WorryTime – a smartphone app to help young people contain their worries to designated periods, thereby freeing up their mind for other activities
- ReachOut Breathe – an app that uses simple visuals to help reduce the physical symptoms of stress and anxiety
- Smiling Mind – developed by psychologists, it is a 'modern meditation' program to bring balance to people's lives and calm the mind via mindfulness meditation.

Jonah had been aware from a very young age that he was attracted to boys, but he was terrified of coming out to his parents. They seemed to be constantly having conversations with friends about how such-and-such's daughter was a good match for him, and how much they were looking forward to having a daughter-in-law and grandchildren.

> He had always strived to please his parents, but
> this pressure was making him constantly tired,
> depressed and anxious.

It is normal for young people to experiment with sexual identities. Some will feel certain early in life that they are attracted to the same sex, whereas some young people will question and experiment for years. Research indicates that around one-fifth of young people are attracted to people of both sexes, of their own sex only, or are not sure.

As health and wellbeing issues for LGBTIQ_ young people are often poorer than others, creating a safe space for discussion is important. If your teenager does come out to you, it's important to stay calm – it's likely that it took an enormous amount of courage to talk to you and it's great that you have created enough of a safe space to have the conversation. Be supportive and love your child for exactly who they are – if you need a little time to understand and get used to the disclosure, say so in a gentle way. The child sitting across from you is still the same child that you have always loved.

> Greta was astounded when her daughter, who was
> in Year 8, casually mentioned that her best friend, a
> child who Greta had known for many years, was self-
> harming. Greta was at first confused, expecting that
> she would have seen the marks on this girl's wrists,
> but her daughter explained that the latest trend was
> to cut on their hips, where marks were less likely to
> be seen. Her daughter concluded the conversation by

stating in a matter-of-fact way that self-harming was
so common she knew more girls who self-harmed
than didn't.

Self-harm is not just attention seeking, though an
individual may use it as a way of letting others know that
they are not coping. Reach Out asked a sample of their
followers for reasons behind their self-harm, and their
responses included:

- to try and express complicated or hidden feelings
- to communicate that they need some support
- to prove to themselves that they're not invisible
- to feel in control
- to get an immediate sense of relief.

It is common for parents who are confronted with
self-harming behaviours to panic and become frightened,
confused or angry. It's critical that you don't share these
feelings with your child – they are already feeling isolated, helpless and desperate, and need your support and
help to get better. Try to stay calm and model that you
can manage *your* difficult emotions. Offer a hug or verbal
affection, and make an appointment to see your GP as
soon as possible.

Chapter 14

Risky business

You have probably never heard of 18-year-old Chance Werner of Cartersville. He died in May 2014 at Lake Allatoona, about 35 miles north-west of Atlanta, Georgia. He and his friends were playing a game down on the docks in which a person would sit in a shopping trolley tied to a pole, then the cart was forcefully pushed off the dock, causing the person to 'pop' out of the cart, and the person would swim to the dock. In what has been described as an accident, Chance decided to be the pole one time. The rope was tied around him instead of the pole. When the trolley was pushed into the lake, it pulled him under and he drowned.

This is a clear example of the teenage male brain not thinking about the consequences of actions and the influence of peer pressure. Research (and my personal life experience) confirms what most parents already know – children become more reckless in the adolescent years, and progressively less reckless in their 20s. I wrote off two cars in my youth and one time, at 17, drank way too much wine and managed to drive home with four drunk friends – unbelievably dumb.

I am not alone when it comes to teenage stupidity. Some young people do incredibly risky things, but now, in the digital era in which we live, they are broadcast far and wide. Stupid, dangerous acts, such as taking selfies on cliff edges or what became known as the 'Tide Pod Challenge' – eating capsules of laundry detergent – that might once have had an audience of two, now have a potential audience of millions, and if one person tries something and puts a video of it online, you can guarantee at least someone will copy them.

It seems clear that adolescents are more likely than other age groups to engage in a number of risky behaviours, including drug and alcohol experimentation, unprotected sex and dangerous driving. For example, the Australian Institute of Criminology reports that for the majority of crimes committed in 2009–10, the most offenders were (surprise, surprise) aged 18 and 19 years old. A research report released by the Australian Institute of Family Studies showed that close to half of 19–20-year-olds had been involved in a vehicle crash, while almost a third had been detected speeding by police at least once. Two-thirds reported driving while very tired. These statistics make sense in light of the fact that 30 per cent of all deaths in young people are as a result of transport accidents, compared to 1 per cent of people aged 25 years or over.

So why did I, at 17, drink cask wine like a fish and then attempt to drive home, without a driver's licence? In Chapter 2 we talked about brain development, and this is the key. During adolescence, emotional arousal is high, peer approval is important and 'sensation seeking' behaviours are common. At the same time, the parts of the brain that help with good decision making and problem solving is not yet developed, and the long-term consequences of behaviours don't tend to feature in these processes. Basically, teens are less likely to slow down and think before they act. This is why US psychologist Dr Laurence Steinberg suggests that we should spend less energy trying to change teenagers' behaviour and more energy trying to change the settings in which they spend time.

Let's look at some common issues that you are likely to be worried about, or indeed dealing with already.

DRUG AND ALCOHOL USE

A report released by Deakin University in 2017 shows a significant drop in alcohol use by teenagers in the last two decades. The study of more than 41 000 teenagers showed that in 1999, almost 70 per cent of teenagers had already drunk alcohol. In 2015 this had dropped by a phenomenal 45 per cent, making teenage non-drinkers the new norm. The average age of first use has risen from 14.4 years to 16.1 years. Deakin University Professor John Toumbourou, known and respected for his many decades of research into teen drug and alcohol use, described this trend as a 'youth-led revolution'. And while in the past there has often been a switch to other drugs if the use of one type of drug or alcohol declines, the research shows that young people are abstaining from the use of other drugs as well.

This is welcome news in the adolescent health and welfare space. The change is attributed to teens and parents being more aware and more educated on how certain substances affect brain development. This includes the guidelines released by the National Health and Medical Research Council in 2009 that recommend that young people under the age of 18 do not drink alcohol at all. These guidelines are based on the fact that young people's brains are still developing; drinking alcohol during this time may damage their brain and lead to health complications later in life. In particular, heavy and extended use of alcohol in adolescence can affect the functioning of the hippocampus, which is responsible for memory and learning, and the prefrontal lobe, which is important for planning, judgement and decision making.

There is, however, still a small group of teenagers who drink at hazardous levels, and so it's important for parents not to let their guard down. The following suggestions have been developed to help delay or minimise the onset of alcohol and drug use in young people:

- Be a good role model. Parents who drink or use drugs are more likely to have children who take up the habit. Drink alcohol in moderation and usually with meals.
- Don't condone drinking prior to age 16, and later if possible, but avoid preaching or controlling behaviour, which is likely to have the opposite effect.

- Improve parent–child relations by using positive reinforcement, listening and communication skills and problem solving.
- Monitor your child's activities – find out where they are, who they are with and what they are doing. Being their glorified taxi driver allows you to meet friends and monitor what is going on.
- Keep your adolescent busy – having an interest such as sport, art, music, dance or drama reduces the likelihood of boredom and consequent unhealthy risk taking.

WHAT IF MY CHILD COMES HOME DRUNK?

It had never crossed Gemma's mind that her youngest son, Adam, was drinking alcohol until early one Saturday morning when she received a phone call from the local police station asking her to pick up her son, who was currently locked up and recovering from acute alcohol abuse. Patrol police in the local park had picked up Adam late the night before – he was alone and abusive when they tried to talk to him, so they bundled him into the back of the van and took him to the station. Adam had been with mates, but when he wouldn't cooperate with them, they left him alone in the park to 'sleep it off'.

Gemma was devastated – she couldn't believe that Adam's friends, who she'd always thought of as reliable and responsible, would just abandon him like that. When she picked up Adam, he still seemed under the influence, and his shirt was ripped and he wouldn't talk. She drove home in tears, wondering how things had gone so wrong so quickly.

So what do you do with your still-drunk teenager?

- Don't panic. Ensure their safety and help them recover. Sobering up takes time, and nothing *but* time will do the job (not even a double cheeseburger!).
- Don't engage them in conversation while they are still drunk. Wait until they have sobered up to get the facts.
- When they are sober (and hopefully remorseful), make it clear that you don't approve, no matter the circumstances, and put in place appropriate consequences (see Chapter 8 for more on consequences).
- Avoid moralising and preaching – this may inspire rebellion rather than agreement (especially if you drink alcohol yourself).
- Talk to them about ways they can deal with peer pressure.
- Make sure lines of communication stay open, and that you know where they are, with whom and what they are doing. They need to earn your trust again.
- Don't put them in a cold shower – you'll just have a cold, wet, drunk teenager.

WHAT ABOUT OTHER DRUGS?

Many parents are frightened and confused by the possibility that their child will be exposed to, and choose to use,
illegal drugs. It doesn't help that media reporting of the
issue is often alarmist and inflammatory, making it seem
that the problem is far more common than it actually is.
The illicit drug most commonly used by 12–17-year-olds is
cannabis, with the 2013 Australian National Drug Strategy
Household Survey showing that around 15 per cent of this
age group had tried cannabis. A 2011 study showed that
3 per cent had tried amphetamines, 3 per cent had tried
ecstasy and less than 2 per cent had tried cocaine or heroin.

When asked why they have smoked cannabis, most
teenagers will say it is because their friends did, and they
wanted to be part of the group. Peer pressure is alive and
well, it seems.

Despite the evidence, some of my clients still can't seem
to fathom the dangers of cannabis, telling me, 'It's green,
natural, grows in the ground and makes me feel good.'
I often point these clients to a 2014 study by Professor
Wayne Hall, an Australian researcher who advises the
World Health Organization, that shows cannabis is
anything but harmless. Professor Hall builds a compelling
case that this drug is highly addictive, increases the risk of
mental illness and is a 'gateway' to the use of harder drugs.

There are no foolproof or guaranteed methods to
prevent your teenager from experimenting with drugs,
but there are techniques that will help to reduce the
likelihood, including the following:

- **Talk to your teenager.** Sounds obvious, but don't underestimate the power of having a communicative and trusting relationship with your child. Share your thoughts and feelings about drugs and be clear on what is acceptable or not.
- **Draw on teachable moments.** Examples are when a character in a favourite show chooses to use drugs, or when a drug overdose at a festival is in the news. Avoid preaching or finger wagging – frame it instead as an open and honest discussion where your teenager can also share some views without fear of judgement.
- **Get to know your teenager's friends.** One of the strongest predictors of use by teenagers is having friends who use drugs. Know where your child is and with whom. Make your house a welcome place for teenagers – get to know them, feed them and, if possible, meet their parents. Minimise the time that they spend in unsupervised groups, because even well-behaved teenagers will occasionally fall victim to the power of groupthink.
- **Be a role model.** This is especially critical in the mid-teen years, when your child will be watching you like a hawk for the opportunity to call out any perceived contradictions between your behaviour and what you are telling them to do. Even parents who attempt to hide their drug use (e.g. by smoking a joint after your child has gone to bed) will usually be found out. Model healthy attitudes to dealing with tough days or negative emotions.

The bottom line is: if you come home and 'bong on', they most likely will too . . .

- **Keep your teen busy.** The main benefits are threefold – this limits your child's availability, gives them an excuse to bow out of activities that may involve drug use ('No thanks, I have a tennis lesson in an hour'), and involves them in community activities that help to develop skills and build resilience.
- **Keep informed.** Find out as much as you can about drugs and alcohol from a reliable and regularly updated source, such as the Alcohol and Drug Foundation (www.adf.org.au) or Family Drug Support Australia (www.fds.org.au).

SEX

Your child is a sexual being from birth, but things really ramp up in the teenage years. The 2013 National Survey of Australian Secondary Students and Sexual Health showed that by Year 10, around one-quarter of Australian teens had engaged in sexual intercourse, rising to one-half in Year 12. The survey also showed a link between drug and alcohol use and sexual behaviours, with almost one in seven young women reporting being drunk or high last time they had sex. A significant number of both girls (28 per cent) and boys (20 per cent) reported having sex when they didn't want to – the most common reason being that they were 'too drunk'. The good news is that contraception was commonly used, and many young people reported not being ready to have sex and feeling proud to say no and mean it.

Another thing to consider is the role of technology in sexual behaviours, which is notable in two key ways. The first is the very high prevalence of sexual experiences using technology, such as sending and receiving sexually explicit messages. While this is now a commonplace part of sexual behaviours between teens, it can get out of hand quickly. Sharing images and feeling pressured to engage in sexual behaviours in real life as a next step can cause problems for teens, not to mention what happens if these images are shared without your child's consent or posted online. Don't rely on school sex education to cover these issues – engage in regular, open and honest discussions with your teen when the opportunities arise.

The second is the role of online pornography in the sexual lives of adolescents. The internet has transformed pornography from something that you need to leave the home to consume via a magazine or film to something that can now be obtained and consumed completely in private – it takes only two clicks to access pornography these days.

A 2017 review of literature by the Australian Institute of Family Studies concluded that almost half of 9–16-year-olds experience regular exposure to sexual images. Boys were more likely to deliberately seek out pornography and to do so more frequently compared to girls.

Pornography is now one of the main sources of sex education for young people in the absence of other information. One of the most significant problems with this is that pornography may portray unhealthy sexual practices, such as not using condoms, and support attitudes that are accepting of sexual and physical violence. The useful and informative Australian website *It's Time We Talked* (www.itstimewetalked.com.au) reports that almost 90 per cent of scenes show physical aggression (including gagging, choking and slapping), and around half show verbal aggression, with the vast majority of the aggression aimed at women. So pornography is not just about sex, but also about gender and power relations.

Accessibility to pornography is unlikely to change, so the best thing we can do is give teenagers the skills and knowledge to navigate this brand-new world of sexual relationships and sex education, and to present alternative stories of sex and relationships. Parents need to step up and be the providers of this information or our kids will go elsewhere. Engage in open communication, discussion and critical thinking about pornography. It's also time to get used to what's out there and lose any sense of shame or embarrassment if we're going to be in touch with our teenagers on this subject, so take an active and informed role.

PIERCINGS, PURPLE HAIR AND TATTOOS

Identity development is a key developmental task in adolescence, and teenagers are expert in trying out different aspects of different identities to see what best fits. For teenagers, this may involve anything from make-up to piercings to dyed hair to dressing like a Goth. Whatever the situation, parents are well advised to avoid criticism or judgement, unless your child's health is at risk.

Piercings (in most states and territories) and tattoos are illegal to perform on anyone under 18 without parental consent. This provides some protection from impulsive decisions in the early teen years for parents who are worried about health risks and later-life regrets. As with most other matters in the teenage years, it is helpful to discuss what your child wants to do and why. Encourage them to wait and see if they are still keen on the idea in a week or a month's time rather than make an immediate decision on something you are unsure about, and let them know they are welcome to come back to you for further discussion. Remember, henna tattoos fade!

As far as dyeing hair goes, and as long as school rules do not prohibit it, my advice is to let your teenager go right ahead (preferably with a non-permanent dye). Many of my teenage clients have elected to dye their hair and, when asked why, usually say something like, 'Changing my hair colour is important to me because I want to change something that isn't permanent. It's a way of expressing myself and my emotions.'

I think the last word on piercing should go to a mother sitting in my room debating this issue with her 14-year-old. 'Every adult is free to have a piercing, Zoe,' she said. 'And I am free to find it ugly.'

GAMING

In 2017, the World Health Organization officially confirmed video game addiction as a mental health disorder. In its revised International Classification of Diseases list for 2018, the organisation added a section on gaming disorder, which is 'characterized by a pattern of persistent or recurrent gaming behaviour'.

According to the report, routine gaming turns into a mental health threat if and when individuals prioritise gaming to the extent that it takes precedence over other interests and activities, and when users can't seem to give up gaming, even when it causes noticeable impairment in personal, family, social, educational, occupational or other important areas of functioning.

Still, parents need to park their video gaming prejudice, avoid buying into the moral panic around technology and realise that the research is clear that the occasional gaming session is not harmful and there is evidence that it can actually be beneficial. Gaming can play a powerful social role for boys in particular – video games are the method by which many boys spend time and engage with their peers and friends. There are also cognitive (e.g. improved hand–eye coordination) and motivational (e.g. feedback that rewards persistence) benefits to gaming.

However, if your child is engaging in all-night marathons and the game transforms into something they simply can't live without, it could be a sign of a larger problem. To get a sense of what is happening, ask your child the following questions:

- What kind of games do you like playing? What do you like about them?
- What's your greatest achievement in a game?
- Do you like playing, or does it get stressful? How do you feel when you stop?
- Is it better playing on your own or with other people (both online or offline)?

- If you are playing with people online, do you know them offline? How important is their friendship to you? Do you talk to them about things other than gaming?
- Is it hard to stop sometimes? Do you feel like you have to keep going, even when it stops being fun?

The content is important (though potentially baffling to anyone outside of the gaming world – 'My greatest achievement is scoring three Symmetra teleporters in a single game!') but look for the feelings and emotions that go with the answers. Is your child anxious, bored or enthusiastic when they answer? Does it feel like they are withholding information or reluctant to go into detail? If your child answers that it is hard to stop playing, that others are relying on them to play in a multiplayer game or that they feel they can't take a break, then gaming may be interfering with their wellbeing.

It's also important to be aware of the increasingly blurry line between gaming and gambling online – for example, are they being drawn into making in-app purchases? It's not hard to rack up a big bill.

While setting time limits and encouraging your child to pursue other activities may work, especially if you catch the problem early enough, serious issues are more likely to require professional help. Stories abound of desperate parents with children who are neglecting personal hygiene and diet, are gaming online all night and become defensive or angry if parents try to set limits. Often there is an underlying problem that is driving the gaming behaviour and needs attention in its own right, such as problems at school or social anxieties.

Ironically, the online environment offers a unique medium for support to those who feel they are addicted to online gaming. If you need some hope that things can get better (or your child needs some support from others who can relate to their addictions), peruse some of the online support groups, such as Wowaholics Anonymous (for those negatively affected by World of Warcraft addiction, https://www.reddit.com/r/nowow), and the Stop Gaming site (https://www.reddit.com/r/StopGaming), which offer real-time support, ideas and alternatives to gaming.

Chapter 15
Family breakdown

There is a fascinating statistic relating to separation and divorce in Australia over the past twenty years. According to the ABS, the median number of years from marriage to separation has remained at around seven to eight years, and from marriage to divorce it has remained at around eleven to twelve years. If we look at these figures alongside the fact that around half of all divorces that occur in Australia involve children under 18 years old, it becomes obvious that many families separate around the time that their children are pre-teenagers or teenagers.

Separation and divorce can bring about intense emotional and personal upheaval for children, including changes to both living arrangements and time spent with parents. All children have a right to continue a meaningful relationship with both parents after separation, when it is safe to do so. Yet the teenage years are also when children naturally begin to separate from their parents and develop independence, and family breakdown can compromise these tasks. To your teenager, it may feel more like you have separated from them.

Teenagers need routine and predictability at home, a secure base from which they can explore their identity and their place in a broader society. Maintaining this secure base and routine can be a formidable task when the family unity is being compromised. How this time of change is negotiated and communicated to the teenager, and the ways in which post-separation parenting arrangements are negotiated, can make a world of difference to how well your child copes during this period.

WHAT DO TEENAGERS SAY ABOUT FAMILY BREAKDOWN?

The findings of a 2011 study by the Australian Institute of Family Studies, which involved interviews with over 600 adolescent children from separated families, showed the following:

- In parenting negotiations, most young people want to be listened to and to play a role in decisions about who they live with, where and when. Importantly, however, not all young people want this. Around one in three did not want to be involved; some felt that this forced them to 'choose' between parents.
- Flexibility in arrangements is high on the adolescent wish list.
- Feeling close to at least one parent is important for a teenager adjusting to changes after parental separation.

- Boys tended to be more affected by the separation and were more likely to hope for reconciliation than girls.
- Adolescent girls were more likely to seek help outside the family to deal with the separation than boys.

Separation may entail other undesirable effects for all involved, such as a drop in standard of living when two households need to be maintained. These things may seem trivial to adults, but may be central to a teen's world that revolves around self-image and the acceptance of peers.

Even though there is a trend towards separating when children are older, family breakdown can still deeply affect young adults. This was demonstrated in a series of text messages between British journalist and former politician Chris Huhne and his son Peter, who was 18 at the time of his parents' divorce in 2011. The text messages, which were published in a national newspaper and can be viewed online in a series of *Guardian* articles, show several attempts by Huhne to express his desire to maintain his relationship with his son. Peter's texts, however, are a painful example of how much anger and vitriol can be felt by older teenagers in the aftermath of a complicated and messy parental relationship breakdown. In one exchange on Christmas Day 2011, Huhne sends a message to wish his son a Happy Christmas and to tell him he loves him. In response, his son comprehensively tells him he hates him and to f*** off.

WHAT SHOULD I BE AWARE OF WHEN SEPARATING?

There are five golden rules to bear in mind during the process of separation:

1. **Avoid conflict in front of your children.** This is important at all stages of a separation. Adolescents are highly sensitive to conflict between parents and the distress that arises from this conflict, even though they may not know it.

2. **Emphasise (repeatedly) to your offspring that they are not responsible for the break-up.** Sometimes it may be emotionally easier for a teenager to blame themselves rather than a parent. This may result in acting out behaviour, or conversely, being overly helpful and compliant. Help them to understand why the break-up occurred.

3. **Make it clear that there's no chance of reconciliation.** Younger adolescents in particular are more likely to hope for reconciliation and feel that things would be better for them if their parents stayed together.

4. **Find time to concentrate on your child's needs and how they are feeling during the separation.** If you are physically or emotionally unable to do so, see if there is a close family friend or relative who can check in on them on a regular basis.

5. **Maintain your expectations in terms of your teenager's behaviour, and make sure these are aligned with your ex-partner's expectations.**

The separation is not an excuse for your teenager to exhibit hurtful, disrespectful or illegal behaviour.

Once the initial shock of the separation has passed, there are other considerations that will help your teenager to manage the new situation:

- Agree with your partner on what is parental business only (e.g. legal and financial arrangements) and what decisions to include the young person in if they wish to be involved (e.g. accommodation and access arrangements, which house they keep their things at, who they spend their birthday lunch/dinner with).
- Avoid using teenagers as messengers or pawns in an ongoing war between you and your ex-partner.
- Your teenager should not be your confidant. It is unfair and unreasonable to use them as a sounding board for your personal problems, particularly those that involve the other parent. Find other ways to unload or blow off steam.
- Try to maintain a normal routine and structure as much as possible. Keep cooking meals, being there when your teenager gets home, hugging them whenever they will let you (or showing affection with words if they won't).
- Respect the fact that the other person is still a parent to the teenager, even though they are no longer your partner. You are entitled to be as angry

as you want about your ex-partner, but talking them down, pointing out their faults, or failing to engage with them to make important parenting decisions can make your teenager feel sad or angry.

- Be aware that teenagers who live in two homes may use this to their advantage. Have an understanding with your ex-partner that you both need to know where your teenager is at all times, even if you find it difficult to communicate about other matters.

If there are problems, seek help from a family mediator or therapist or, if necessary, a family lawyer as soon as possible. At the time of writing, ex-partners must move through a mediation process before any legal processes occur, with the exception of cases where family violence is present. This allows families the opportunity to make decisions about parenting plans and other post-separation matters in a non-adversarial environment.

THE THIRD WHEEL

It's likely that there will be a third person at the negotiating table when it comes to figuring out parenting and accommodation arrangements – your teenager. Young people often have so much gear to drag around, be it sports gear or musical instruments, or the right clothing or make-up, that moving between two households becomes a real challenge. They also have a lot of extracurricular and social activities to deal with. This can make moving regularly from house to house more difficult and stressful than when they were younger.

You and your ex-partner need to face the fact that your teenager's preference may be to have a post-separation parenting arrangement of zero time with either parent (just like any other teenager!). You are unlikely to be the centre of their universe in the same way as when they were little. Think about what *they* need, not what you need.

Remember, teenagers tend to have a black and white view of the world. They may side with the parent who they feel closest to and who they think has been wronged in the separation process. So be prepared for a rough ride. You can't expect them to see things with an adult perspective.

I'M REPARTNERING – WILL MY TEENAGER GET ALONG WITH MY NEW PARTNER?

You can be hopeful, but don't expect teenagers to warm to or even want to be friends with your new partner. They may feel an intense loyalty to the other parent, and they may not want to compromise this by being seen tolerating or enjoying time with the new partner. Like most other things in your teenager's life, you can't force them to feel or do anything. Be patient, communicate, and accept that a relationship between your teenager and your new partner may take a long time to establish.

If your teenager is rude or disrespectful, however, they need to know that this is unacceptable, just as it is with any other person that they know.

I'M NOT COPING . . .

During or after separation, it's common to have phases where you feel irreparably fragile, and having a teenager lurching around the house, singing songs and eagerly talking about their hot date is not always a great self-esteem booster for a parent in crisis. So it's critical to look after yourself over this period. Here are a few strategies:

- Keep active and try to remain social. You'll need the support of friends.
- It's normal to experience waves of emotion and grief. It may not feel like it, but the grief will pass. Be especially kind to yourself in the down times.
- Try to avoid excessive alcohol or other drug use. It may help you cope in the short-term, but your problems will still be there in the morning.
- Hold your own hand when you fall asleep at night – you'll be surprised how comforting this can be.

It's also important to let your teenager know that feeling lots of different emotions at different times is normal and that this may be magnified at times of separation or divorce. Crying is a normal reaction and a good release.

Mental illnesses such as anxiety are shown to be more common among young people from single-parent or blended families. Where the separation is difficult and characterised by conflict, or where money is a problem, the risk of mental illness is higher. It doesn't mean that mental illness is inevitable or long lasting, but it does mean that parents in these circumstances need to be especially alert to the warning signs (see Chapter 13).

Finally, remember that one day your teenager will be an adult and may tell you exactly what they thought of the way you managed these challenges. Think about what you would like to hear, and work towards it. There will always be matters outside of your control, including the relationship between your child and their other parent – but that is their responsibility, not yours! Keep moving forward and use the ideas in this chapter to create the best life you can. Things will get easier.

Afterword

AND THE FINAL WORD GOES TO...

A good friend of mine, Elsa, has a daughter named Katie. At 14, Katie was a determined teenager who was certain that she already had all the skills and knowledge she needed to face the world alone.

One day, after multiple fruitless attempts to ring Katie and find out where she was, Elsa became frustrated at her daughter's obstinacy. This was only amplified by the text that Katie sent her some hours later, which simply said, 'Yes?'

Exasperated, Elsa replied, 'Answer your phone!'

Katie immediately shot back, 'Answer my call for freedom!'

The good news is, in a few short years, everyone's wishes will be granted.

Resources

adf.org.au

The Alcohol and Drug Foundation is a nationwide organisation committed to preventing alcohol and other drug harms in Australia. It has excellent, evidence-based resources for young people, parents and the broader community.

raisingchildren.net.au/teens/teens.html

The Raising Children Network has information and tips on raising healthy pre-teens and teenagers.

commonsensemedia.org

Common Sense Media improves the lives of kids and families by providing independent reviews, age ratings and other information about all types of media.

healthyfamilies.beyondblue.org.au/age-13

This website provides information on raising resilient young people, and common mental health problems.

parents.au.reachout.com

Reach Out for Parents helps parents support their teenagers through everyday issues and tough times.

esafety.gov.au

This website provides online safety education and a complaints service for cyberbullying and illegal content.

fds.org.au

Family Drug Support Australia offers 24/7 information and referral.

There are also parenting help lines in each state or territory if you wish to talk to someone:

Australian Capital Territory 02 6287 3833
New South Wales 1300 130 052
Queensland/Northern Territory 1300 301 300
South Australia 1300 364 100
Tasmania 1300 808 178
Victoria 132 289
Western Australia 1800 654 432

Acknowledgements

Michael Carr-Gregg

I'd like to extend my profound gratitude to my co-pilot Elly Robinson for strapping in and taking this third excursion with me into the world of adolescents and parenting.

I have actually run out of words to describe the amazing Ali Watts, so I'll just say thank you and all hail our literary panelbeater par excellence. Thank you also to Amanda Martin and the rest of the team at Penguin.

Thanks too much go to both my wife, Therese, and our sons, Christopher and Rupert – neither of whom are juvenile delinquents.

Elly Robinson

To my funny, clever, adventurous, affectionate and fiercely independent daughter. I wrote this just to see the look on your face. Love always.

And thank you to the team at Penguin Random House for your help, encouragement and persistence.

Index

the
PRINCESS
BITCHFACE
SYNDROME 2.0

Surviving
adolescent
girls

MICHAEL CARR-GREGG
and ELLY ROBINSON

If you feel like you're losing control when it comes
to parenting your daughter, it's time to grab back
the reins with this phenomenal Australian bestseller –
over 100 000 copies sold.

Surviving
adolescent
boys

the
**PRINCE
BOOFHEAD**
SYNDROME

MICHAEL CARR-GREGG
and **ELLY ROBINSON**

The long-awaited, highly anticipated companion
volume to *The Princess Bitchface Syndrome* – the
must-have manual for all parents of teenage boys.